TINY HOUSE BASICS

Living the Good Life in Small Spaces

Joshua Engberg and Shelley Engberg
Foreword by Derek "Deek" Diedricksen, Bestselling Author of *Microshelters*

PRAISE FOR TINY HOUSE BASICS

"**OUTSTANDING!** Josh and Shelley's book not only gives us a new perspective on what happens behind the TV cameras, but more importantly, it gives us a behind-the-curtain view into the realities and challenges of building a tiny house. The format is easy to understand, thorough, and a must read for anyone who's even THINKING about building a tiny house. The good news is that I now have another resource to add to my tiny house library. The bad news is that I'll have to cancel my own plans to write a book because I think they've covered it all!"

– Michelle Boyle
 Writer at My Empty Nest & My Tiny Perch

"Tiny House Basics gives you a front row seat to the mindset and process of becoming a tiny house dweller for the long haul."

– Steven Harrell
 Owner of Tiny House Listings

"Shelley and Joshua offer **GREAT ADVICE** on how to make a tiny house work for two. They demonstrate how a strong foundation and good communication are essential—not only in building a tiny house, but in living and thriving in one!"

– Alek Lisefski
 From The Tiny House Project

"It is one thing to read a book about the theory of a transition. It is quite another to read one based on someone's personal testimony of transition. Joshua and Shelley have nailed it in regards to balancing tips with case study. Their emphasis on being realistic in all things - from design to daily living - is both important and inspiring. In my 9 years of being active in the modern tiny house movement I have not yet read such a well thought out book for those at all stages of the "going tiny" process."

– Andrew M. Odom
Tiny r(E)volution, Author, Speaker, and Practical Strategist

"Tiny House Basics is HONEST ABOUT THE JOURNEY. Joshua and Shelley get you thinking about what you can do to live a little simpler, even if you're not building a tiny house."

– Mario Soto
Tiny House, MD.

"Andrew and I live and work together full time in our tiny house, and we know from firsthand experience what challenges these circumstances present. Shelley and Joshua totally get it too and have learned the secrets to a successful and thriving relationship in a small space. In Tiny House Basics they eloquently share valuable tips that anyone can greatly benefit from, whether they live tiny or not."

– Gabriella Morrison
Tiny House Build

"With the CREATIVITY, QUALITY AND SUCCESS of their tiny house build, Joshua and Shelley of Tiny House Basics have proven themselves to be experts in the tiny house community."

– Jewel Pearson
Tiny House Trailblazers

TO OUR LOVING AND DESERVING PARENTS:

Eric and Helene Engberg and Julie and James Mulligan. You guys have supported us throughout this wild ride in more ways than one. We are forever grateful.

PS: This book is best enjoyed with a shrimp cocktail.

CONTENTS

FOREWORD

By: Derek "Deek" Diedricksen

*Author, Designer, Builder, YouTube host of "RelaxshacksDOTcom",
and former host of HGTV's "Tiny House Builders"*

I'LL BE HONEST in initially stating that I have a rather short attention span. Add to that the fact that I travel to teach workshops, speak at tiny home festivals and shows, build and design tiny structures, and have written a string of books on the subject matter, and you might start to see a painted picture leading to the fact that, in reality, I don't impress easily anymore. It happens. It bums me out a bit too, as I realize I've become a bit jaded while so constantly immersed in the small housing scene. These days, having personally filmed and toured hundreds of small structures, and additionally having spent the night in dozens upon dozens of them, it takes a heck of a lot to turn my head, and it takes far more to "wow" me. Well, only a couple years back, during a late night tiny house online binge, I stumbled upon a funky, modern, bright, fun, and daring little house that turned out to be owned, built, and designed by, yep, Joshua and Shelley Engberg. This one had all the things I loved: open space, an abundance of windows, bright and selective pops of color, and one of the cooler kitchen and entertainment spaces I've yet to see. Furthermore, beyond all that, it just looked, felt, and, well, *was*, different from so many houses I had come across. The 8' accordion window didn't hurt either. For a moment, as so happens every now and again, the jaded veil was lifted, and I was both

inspired and given a hint of the feelings I used to get when I was seeing my very first tiny houses well over two decades back.

It's funny how things sometimes work out, connect, and "happen." Fast forward to the present, and things have gone from my seeing a mere glimpse of the Engberg's home, to us getting together for dinner in Massachusetts on their US road trip, later walking the streets of Los Angeles with them in search of street-truck burritos, to eventually actually working and building with this duo. Somehow, at some point,

as often happens in this scene, things turned from a passing mutual admiration in architecture, to a friendship with this opposite coast duo. I ain't complainin'. Not only are the Engberg's good, honest, and adventurous people, but they are a wealth of tiny house design, decor, and construction knowledge as well- as you'll soon see. So take this text-journey with them, allow them to lead you through the ropes, tricks, tribulations, and perils of designing micro dwellings, and realize that through it all, you're in good hands.

INTRODUCTION

Who Lives In These Tiny, So-Called "Tiny Houses?

TINY HOUSES are like the kittens of regular-sized houses; they're small and adorable and are oozing with charm in their little bite-sized frames. We can't get enough of seeing these little guys on TV and on social media, but who are the people actually living in them? Many may want to stereotype people living in a tiny house as those with either no dreams or jobs, earthy folks who want to only live off the land and make their own essential oils and shampoo and play in their gardens all day. This was a common stereotype, initially. Sad to say, that's what came to mind when we thought of tiny houses back before we knew what they really were. Fast forward several years and here we are, now living in a Tiny House for some years now and we love it! Here is a little background on who we are, who we were, and what made us decide to take the tiny plunge.

We are a young couple in our early thirties who live in the San Francisco Bay Area. We got married in 2011, and after we were married, moved in together to our 1,300-square foot rental house. We were what seemed like your common newly married couple who lived in an expensive area, working full-time, and more often than not, working much more than

full-time. We've always loved going out to new restaurants and trying new cocktail bars, regularly seeing music shows, and getting away for some good, solid camping and off-roading. We never had the interest to buy a home, since 1) they're so very expensive in the San Francisco Bay Area; and 2) we didn't know where we wanted to put roots down for long enough to be trapped in one city for years and years this early on. So, for us, renting seemed like the best option for the time being. We first learned about tiny houses while out to dinner with friends in Berkeley one evening. They were also a young couple without kids who mentioned wanting to downsize to a tiny house. We asked, "What in the world is a tiny house?!" They showed us a couple of pictures, and at that time it didn't seem they were any larger then maybe 100 square feet. We thought it looked cute because it was basically a little dollhouse on wheels. However cute, we initially saw them as a ridiculous idea for any couple to be in such a small space! Occasionally, we would stumble across one on the Internet and jokingly send it to our friends, still thinking those

little things were ridiculous. A couple years went by, and more and more we were tired of paying high rent to horrible landlords; the prices were only increasing for rents and homes to buy.

Life started feeling very much like a double-edged sword to be working so much to pay for a house we didn't own, were never at, and didn't have time to enjoy because all our time was spent working to pay for the place to live in; yet, it didn't feel like we were doing much living at all. Even if we did buy a home, it would come with the same time-consuming responsibilities that we already had, plus many more! Either way, the result would be that we worked and worked and worked and had a house to show for it, but what about a life? When do we get to live a life more than just two days a week? We have so many other ways we want to spend our time doing things we love and enjoy, including volunteer work helping others. How do we get to work less and still survive while being able to enjoy life a little? Was it even possible in the San Francisco Bay Area, or did we need to consider moving out of the area entirely? Of course, that wasn't ideal either; our families, good friends, and jobs were all here. Relocating would be a big effort, but it wasn't off the table. The life of living to work was never our goal. We, in fact, wanted to work to live, so we could enjoy our youthful energy now as opposed to enjoying more time and having far less energy later in life.

On our second anniversary, we went to our family cabin in Washington state at the foot of Mount Rainier National Park; one of us had never seen it, while the other grew up going to it. Even so, it had been years since going to the cabin. The cabin was roughly 600 square feet, built out of solid wood logs with two small rooms, a tiny bathroom (even smaller than our current tiny house bathroom), a small but functional kitchen and living room, an awesome large cobblestone fireplace, and a large beautiful outdoor deck that looked out onto a small waterfall among the evergreens. It was so peaceful being in its gorgeous nature setting; we were loving the small space even as it rained half the time, causing us to stay in. It was so cozy, and even better, it was easy to keep clean and orderly, something we've both always struggled at in our larger space. The size felt so beyond comfortable and doable, and felt like more than enough space; this realization was a turning point for us.

When we first got married, we wanted a bigger house with more space to have friends and family stay when need be and to entertain more people. We had what we thought were big dreams. Of course, as time went on, we quickly learned that even if we did attain this larger house, we still would have to maintain and clean the thing and pay the expensive utility bill that would come with our larger "dream home." That aspect was not appealing. Can't we just get a sweet, big house with a cleaning and maintenance crew given to us so we can go play all the time? Since like most people we have to work to pay our bills, that pipe dream was off the table. Getting back to reality, we really started feeling more and more that a smaller, more maintainable space would be better for us. Spending that time in the cabin made us realize how much we were craving to have less junk. We just wanted to get back to basics.

About six months after staying in the cabin, one night we stumbled across the documentary "TINY: a story about living small" on Netflix; we had completely forgotten about tiny houses. As we watched the documentary, we saw that there were, in fact, regular people downsizing to live in them, and what was even more appealing was that the tiny houses were being built in larger sizes than we thought was even possible! It was a lightbulb moment for us. We looked at each other and said, "We can live in one of those!" By this point, we were so sick of feeling like the small amount of spare time we did have was often needed to clean the house and the garage, care for the yard, and constantly try to organize and maintain our many items we had accumulated. We more and more felt buried by our possessions and buried by the time we needed to spend to maintain them, making us ready to purge and have less stuff closing in on us. We wanted more freedom. How did we get caught in the typical trap that more stuff and a larger home means more happiness? It was clear to us that it didn't mean more happiness, but meant more frustration as we were craving to get out of our trapped routine and go see more. We wanted to explore more and help people more and just stop spinning our wheels for an unsatisfying lifestyle. After watching the documentary and thinking we certainly can do this, we made up our minds then that we were going to work hard and fast to accomplish it and give this lifestyle a try. Why not? Why not try: we're adventurous and spontaneous and enjoy trying new things. It would be a unique challenge and we were up to it. We then started researching day and night for a few months, while meanwhile selling off tons of stuff that we didn't need or use. We had made our minds up that we were going to do this and not stop until we got it. We had never felt so certain about a goal for our living situation until now! This was it, it was going to get us to a state of more contentment and a better peace of mind, while allowing us to live a more meaningful and fulfilling life—plus our money was going to go much further!

When we initially told our family and friends about our grand plan, they didn't understand it or how we would be able to live comfortably in a much smaller space. There was also skepticism about us making it happen. Of course, we couldn't blame them; it did sound bizarre at that time, as tiny houses and small spaces were a newer shift in thinking in America and tiny houses were just starting to pop up. We didn't take it as being unsupportive; it was just so unfamiliar, and we knew it would be an educational process. If the shoe had been on the other foot, we probably would have been skeptical about it as well. We were determined to make this happen and show our family and friends that it could be done and designed in a way that didn't feel cramped and didn't leave us feeling like we were missing out and yearning to have many of our sold off items back. We had several details on our list that we knew we needed to have included in our small space? One large detail was that we would still have the ability to entertain comfortably in our new small space. We didn't need a large house to have friends and family over to have a good time. After all, everyone ends up in one room or area, anyway. We were done with feeling tricked by society telling us we needed specific things in order to obtain happiness. Who set this standard anyways?! Many other countries in Europe and Asia have been living in small spaces for ages and think nothing of it. So why here in America are we wound so tight that we have to measure success by the size of the home we live in or the car we drive? Admittedly, we had been wrapped up in that mentality as well. When it's what surrounds us, it can be very hard to shift our thinking. The Tiny House movement is a growing effort to shift our thinking, and measure success by our level of happiness rather than measuring our happiness by the items we possess.

Of course, this is not to say that in order to be happy you must purge all your items and downsize to a tiny house. Everyone and every situation is different. We're all unique and will all have unique living situations to fit our individual needs and comfort levels. Simplifying may very well be downsizing from 5,000 square feet to 2,000 square feet if that's what fits your situation and needs. Simplifying is a very personal process and is as individual as each of us.

Throughout this book, we will talk about our process of downsizing and building a tiny house, some dos and don'ts we've learned after living in our tiny house for several years, as well as things we would have done differently. We'll explain the full process, from how to get started when buying your trailer to finishing décor touches, and give you full access to our raw experience thus far from a couple who are far from being minimalists. We'll show you ways to store items in a decorative but functional way to save space that can be applied to any size home. You'll be surprised just how much can fit into only 374 square feet! We'll also help guide you as to what your expectations can be regarding price, finding land, and even timelines of self-builds as well as professional builds. We have lots to cover and hope in the end you'll have a better idea of what type and size tiny house fits your needs best.

CHAPTER 1

Making The Decision To Go Tiny

WE ARE SHELLEY AND JOSHUA, and we and our two dogs have been living in a 374-square foot tiny house for a few years now. As unbelievable as it may seem, we love it. However, if you had told either of us while we were in college that we were going to one day live in something no larger than an Ikea kitchen layout (and be happy and content), we would have dropped on the floor laughing and probably would have ridiculed you It was incredibly unlikely. Like many young couples, we had large aspirations when we were in our college years. We were going to be greatly successful, own a massive house with five bedrooms, three bathrooms, a pool, and who knows what else. We dreamed about possibly another vacation house or two with amazing cars. This desire came with a struggle.

We fell into the trap of finding jobs we hated that paid well in order to squeeze in vacations. Of course, when you're nineteen, nobody tells you how much work and time all of that will take to attain. Also, nobody told us how exhausting it would be to get there, and how much of that fictional life that we had created in our heads would be put on hold while

we worked tirelessly to get to what we thought was the top. As young adults, though, even if anybody had tried to tell us, we wouldn't have listened anyway. Some things we just had to learn on our own through our own life experiences and painful lessons.

Here is a little background on us both:

Shelley's Story

I went to college right out of high school to get an art degree in interior design. I always loved anything design-related. As a young girl, I was strangely obsessed with decorating shows and design showrooms of all types. I had the constant itch to want to create a cozy and stylish space. In our own house growing up, I was always trying to talk my parents into buying certain art pieces or redoing the living room every couple of months. I couldn't help but walk into people's homes and instantly redesign and knock down walls in my head so they could have more efficient space. I loved many styles and textures and still do to this day. I come from a humble background; my father owned a small painting company with a handful of employees that my mom helped him with, while they raised my two older brothers and me.

My goal in going to college was to start small with a staging company, then work up to commercial and/or high-end residential design, and either work for a high-profile design firm or start my own. While in school, I worked at a couple of places doing design-related jobs, but the school loans were beyond my low-paying wage. Nearing the end of my schooling, I got a job offer at a large utility company making a great wage, more than any design company was going to offer me being right out of college. So I took it to get some headway on school loans. After five years with the company, I felt like I had had enough. The job was torture, and I felt my soul was being sucked right out of me as I commuted four hours a day, sat at a desk, which I hated, and oftentimes had to work mandatory overtime at an already intense job. I was already burned out. It only took five years... How was I going to keep going at this pace and still have the energy to enjoy life outside of a building? I had no time to even spend the money I made, barely any time for a vacation. This isn't at all what I had envisioned as a meaningful and happy life.

After Joshua and I got engaged, I quit my job to work part-time helping with his business. This was something we discussed at length for a long time before taking the step to quit my current job. This was a huge step for me; many thought I was crazy for quitting this job at such a desirable-to-work-for company. Although it was scary giving it up, it was also exhilarating. I've never liked being bored, so this was a new challenge that excited me. Little did I know at that time that it would be one of the best decisions I made.

Joshua's Story

Out of high school, I went to a technical school for aeronautical mechanics and repair at Oakland International Airport, where I spent the next couple of years learning the ins-and-outs of working on airplanes. I graduated at the top of my class on the dean's list, and I was then set on advancing my career in the aviation field. My next "goal" was to pursue a degree in mechanical engineering at a highly-rated aeronautical university. However, before I made that drastic decision that would occupy another four or more years of my life, I decided to take the summer off and think about what I really wanted to do with my life. After graduating the academy, I was hired to work further with the school by preparing airplanes that were purchased in St. Louis and shipped to Oakland to be used in instruction for future students. During this time the industry was changing rapidly, and the loyalty that the big airlines had towards the crews that kept the airplanes in the air was almost nonexistent. I began to question if I would even like to take this career further.

To this day, I still have a deep love for aviation and the field of mechanics, but I decided ultimately that I didn't want to slave away for a lifetime, giving my career to an industry that would not uphold its loyalty to me when times got tough. So, I pursued another career. In the mid-2000s the real estate market was booming, and I decided to join my family business by becoming a real estate agent. Growing up, I watched my parents transition through different careers before they got into real estate. My mother and father both worked hard while taking care of my older brother and me. My father worked full-time in the uniform industry, and my mother, while taking care of us, worked as a house cleaner and made porcelain dolls on the side as a hobby and a side job to support her love for garage sales and deal hunting. All these skills they developed through different jobs and hobbies led them into real estate. For me, real estate was a far cry from my passion of working on airplanes, metal fabrication, and welding, but it was still very enjoyable work.

The best part for me was working with people and finding that perfect dream home, wondering what kind of home would be my perfect place. The market at the time was great: interest rates were low, and virtually anybody could buy a home, even someone like myself who was fresh out of school with good credit and not much else. Of course, hindsight is 20/20, but in the present, you can only make the best decision based on the information you have at hand, and the information at that time encouraged everyone to buy a house, whether you could truly afford it or not. So, I did what many Americans did: I bought a house because I thought it was the right thing to do. I mean, I had the credit and the mortgage payment was low, so why not? Like so many people believed (and sadly still believe), I felt that I could figure the rest out as time went on. Time didn't seem to go on too long, and twenty-four months later, my mortgage doubled! As one of the early ones in the mortgage crisis, I lost my house. There was no way I could afford to keep the payment up when it doubled overnight. Like many, I thought I was ahead of the game and had my dream home, and after only a few years I lost it to the bank. I just felt hopeless and back at square one. A short time later, while still practicing real estate, I noticed a trend of foreclosed houses coming back on the market, but needing repairs and preservation before being resold. I made a transition in the field of real estate from selling to preserving these houses while they were on the market. After losing my own house, I could fully relate to what people were going through when they had to move out of their own houses. My job then became to help them with that transition and to repair and preserve the house while it went back on the market. Over the course of the next few years, I was servicing and

preserving homes across the San Francisco Bay Area in over sixty-five cities, which equated to about 35,000 miles a year of driving with work days that lasted, on average, over fourteen hours.

Starting Our Life Together

After we got married, the business was busier than ever for the next couple of years. This meant long and demanding work days, and worst of all, it meant we rarely got to see each other. One of the memories from that time that sticks out is waking up very early and rushing out to beat rush hour traffic. The depression of saying bye to each other while hoping we would both get to see each other later at a decent hour... A typical day often included heading out to work extra early due to the nature of the business, which included driving through up to fifteen or more cities a day performing heavy-duty tasks with a crew. We also did a lot of driving through cities documenting the state of different properties. We had the goal that sooner, rather than later, the business would essentially run itself, with us having to do some light managing. As more time went on, however, the clients started to get more demanding of our time and attention; we started to see more clearly that our goal of being less hands-on was getting further out of reach. Our already fourteen-hour workdays were not leaving any extra time to do the things we enjoyed that kept us sane.

Regardless of the increasing pressure we were dealing with, we decided we had taken on too much and decided to start scaling back little by little. At this time, we still weren't thinking of going tiny; we were just thinking of our sanity. One of the biggest frustrations with owning and running a business was that we never seemed to be able to take a break. Vacations were a mere dream that never happened due to how demanding the business was. Even getting away for a couple of nights for our anniversaries was tough. When we finally were able to get away for an anniversary in Santa Barbara, we had a real turning point. At this point, we had let a couple clients go, as the business was starting to get very cutthroat and the work was becoming more intense and demanding as the phone would never stop ringing. We got to a breaking point with most of our large clients as the expectations had become unreal and left us feeling lifeless. We scaled back further and only kept smaller clients; it would be something that just the two of us could do and handle without having to manage a crew.

Not too long after scaling back we started to feel a little freer and like ourselves again! There was still one problem, though: we still felt burdened by our expensive rent and started realizing we didn't need this extra space. Our home was only around 1,300 square feet and even still, we only used a quarter of it. Most of our house just stored our junk and toys that we bought but never had to time to use. Our house was essentially an expensive storage unit. Our young adult dream of a massive house and all the other luxuries really started to change. We didn't want more stuff, we wanted more time. More time to enjoy the things we truly loved and valued, like spending time growing our relationships with our families and friends, volunteering in our bible education work, and traveling and camping.

We realized that we didn't need to make a small fortune to do these things; we needed to work smarter, not harder. It was around this time when we realized that we needed to cut our living expenses, and the largest one was our house. Since prices in the San Francisco Bay Area were only increasing and our business was here, we couldn't just up and leave and start our new lives in a new, less expensive area. This is when we started to recall our friends telling us years ago about tiny houses. It's also when we discovered that tiny houses didn't have to be as small as we had thought! After watching the documentary *"Tiny"* on Netflix and seeing how well they could be laid out and how practical they could be, we were hooked! This was going to be how we achieved our simplified lifestyle without giving up everything. With our backgrounds in design and metal fabrication, the ideas starting flowing on how we were going to create a comfy and spacious-feeling tiny house.

Saying out loud that we were going to do it was the easy part, but making the actual decision was a bit different. At first, our adrenaline started pumping, seeing that this was something so different and exciting! Freedom was right around the corner...or so we thought.

- Could actually do it?

- What size would we live in?
- What size is practical so we can be comfortable and not feel like we're squeezing by each other all the time?
- How was it going to be with dogs? What about closet space, since we both have both dress and casual clothes?
- What about our king bed that we've grown accustomed to and had no intention of giving up? What about our garage full of tools?
- Can we really do it as inexpensively as some have said they did?
- How long will it take us to build it ourselves?
- Is building it ourselves going to be practical, since we still have to work?
- How much of a strain is it going to be while paying expensive rent AND investing into building our tiny house?

So many questions were coming to mind. Even the thought of buying a nice travel trailer crossed our minds. One problem with full-time RV/trailer living for us was that it didn't have custom options that we could put into a tiny house. We still wanted something that felt very solid with normal home-feeling touches; tiny houses were still stick construction and that was something we were very drawn to. Also, we could have things like an awesome bi-fold accordion window. Stairs in our little home? A kitchen with

normal-sized appliances? Yes please! We knew that while it would certainly be an adjustment, a tiny house is what would best suit our needs. One of the bigger talking points for us was, "Oh boy, what will our friends and family think? Will they be supportive or try and talk us out of it?"

We were both raised going camping with our families, and we loved the simplicity that camping offered. We would always pack up our vehicles with only the essential items, and we lacked nothing for the week or two we were in the woods. This love of camping continued into adulthood, where we stepped it up a few notches to extreme off-roading and even more remote campsites in the wilderness. This type of camping became more refined as the years went on. We would travel on very difficult off-road terrain and trails, packed up with all our necessary recovery gear and tools in case we broke down on the trail. In addition to that, we needed to have adequate items for setting up camp at the end of the day, so we could truly relax before we did it all over again the next day. By refining the amount of gear we brought and actually needed, we lessened our packing every trip. We eventually built a custom off-road trailer to handle all the terrain our 4Runner would go through; this off-road trailer ended up becoming our basecamp between trails; our little "vacation tiny house," you could say. Having a comfortable camp has always been an inspiration

for us to strive to live more simply, and when we first thought about downsizing to a real tiny house, we realized we could use many of the things we learned growing up camping and off-roading to simplify our life to just what we needed.

We love camping and off-roading but we didn't want to feel like we're living a full-on camping life indefinitely. Is living tiny going to feel like we were camping 24/7? One of the big questions for most couples going tiny is: is living in such a small space going to affect our relationship negatively? The biggest fear that crossed our minds was, what if we invest all this time and money and it doesn't work out, what if it feels too tiny and we want out shortly after?

We got right to researching and did so for about six months, day and night. We researched by watching YouTube videos and looking on Pinterest and Googling anything and everything related to tiny houses. During this time, we were able to see what we did and didn't like in a tiny house.

Are You Ready Quiz

- Do you *really* use all the space you have in your home?
- Do you have a room or closet that is only used for storage that houses items never used?
- Do you really use every single thing you own on a monthly or seasonal basis?
- Are there pieces of clothes or items you own that you haven't used in the past six months to a year?
- Do you think you can live in half the square footage you do now if it created more time to spend doing things you enjoy?
- What appeals to you the most about living with less space and less square footage?
- What is more important: more time or more stuff?
- Can you recall immediately what's stored in areas less-used in your house without digging through them?
- Do you spend more time maintaining your toys than you do using them?
- Does the thought of enjoying your life now appeal to you more vs. potentially having to wait many years to start enjoying it?

CHAPTER 2

Planning: Research

RESEARCHING and downsizing for your tiny home will be one of the most exciting but stressful—and sometimes frustrating—parts of the whole process. This is where the dreaming and imagining start to become real, and the decisions that need to be made can at times feel overwhelming. Even so, we cannot stress enough to RESEARCH, RESEARCH, RESEARCH. Doing your homework is important, even though it can be very time-consuming and seem endless at times. You will certainly not regret spending the extra time on this part. With the movement ever growing, the wealth of information is increasing. So where do you start?

Research, Research (and for good measure, probably some more research)

Size

The first step is figuring out what size is practical for you and/or anyone else who is going to be living in the space. When we were trying to figure out what size would suit us best, we started by watching every YouTube video possible, repeatedly. The movement was still very new, so there weren't any real examples of places we could go to see inside one. So, we

had to get creative and carefully watch videos and study pictures to really get a sense of the space with people in it. This may also be the case for you depending on where you live and the availability of tiny houses near you; really looking and studying what the space looks like and how people interact in their smaller space will be helpful.

Being realistic about what size you will need to be comfortable in a space is key. Going tiny or downsizing doesn't mean you need to be extreme. A lot of people will have very strong opinions as to what a tiny house is and means and what size you need to be living in to be categorized as a tiny house. However, the goal is not to just fit into a category, but to be practical about your needs.

The size will depend on how many people will be living in the space and what you need to accomplish in your daily routine. If you are one person, you can very well have an easier time adapting to one on the smaller side. If you're a couple of people or even a small family, then it can get a bit more complicated as the planning and decisions will depend on each person's needs. Do you plan to travel with your tiny house? If so, then something to think about is how often you will be towing, which will affect your decision on size. For instance, having something 28 feet and above

will be harder to tow on a regular basis. Due to the construction of tiny houses and their height, the larger the tiny house, the more weight to be towed. If you are looking to do as we did, which is having it as our main base camp and traveling outside of the tiny house, then you can look at the larger/longer tiny homes. We intended on our tiny house to be a semi-permanent setup. We never intended on traveling with it, but rather traveling because of it. Based on what we've seen and the feedback of those traveling in their tiny home, if you plan to travel regularly with it, you may want to consider no larger than 24 feet. Even so, many who travel regularly seem to think that 20 feet or under is a better size. If you plan to travel every other month or so, then the larger size of around 24 feet would still be doable; it'll just be slower towing (think towing a wall). Another thing to keep in mind for traveling is your roof line. We live in a very tree-filled area. While the height limit due to freeway overpasses is 13 feet, 6 inches, you still want to think about your terrain. For example, since our area is so heavily tree-filled and we wanted a shed roof— meaning it slants to one side—we made sure that the higher side would

be on the driver's side for towing, as the trees that would get close would be on the passenger side of the truck and tiny house. Same if you're planning on traveling with your tiny house often, you want to take into consideration and research what type of roof line would be the best.

For those who are like us, who plan on staying put for longer periods and are two or more people, you can look into what's considered a "larger" tiny house of 28 feet or longer. For us, this seemed like the sweet spot. Just a few things that made us consider this size was that it would allow a good amount of space for us to have normal amenities, such as an apartment-sized kitchen with an eating bar on the inside and outside of our 8-foot accordion/bi-fold window above it, a good-sized bathroom, and also a space to fit a normal sofa and a king-sized bed. These were some of the more important things for us in choosing this size. If you are a small family looking to go tiny, then perhaps 32 feet and above may be more suitable in order to have separate sleeping spaces and more space for storage. Another question to ask yourself is whether you would like a sleeping loft, or if you would like to have your bed on the same level. What exactly is a sleeping loft, you might ask, and how is it different from a regular loft or bedroom? When in a tiny house, there will be height limitations to the overall height of the structure of 13 feet 6 inches due to the fact that they are on wheels and need to abide by legal road limits. Staying under this height means that you can go under interstate overpasses. If you decided to go over that height you would need to get transport permits. Keeping your tiny house within legal limits will mean that you will likely need to have a shorter sleeping loft, as in one you cannot stand up in it. For instance, our sleeping loft is 4 feet 3 inches on the high side, and 3 feet 6 inches on the low side since we have a slanted shed roof line. A sleeping loft will be a crawl-in loft for the majority of cases. You can, however, adjust the loft to the height to fit whatever your needs are during building.

If you're not a fan of the idea of a sleeping loft, then something longer to accommodate a bed on the same level may be a better fit. There's also the option of a gooseneck style, which some may know as a fifth wheel. This would allow you to have just a couple of steps leading up to a bedroom area, rather than having to climb stairs or a ladder. Another option for those wanting to have a bed on the ground level is to have a Murphy bed, or even a bed that slides out from under an area that can be utilized as another usable space for something, such as an office or raised living room.

Amenities Needed

When considering what size you'll want, you'll also want to consider what appliances are must-haves for you. This is when a good, honest self-examination comes into play. For instance, in the beginning, our must-haves list looked something like this.

We had planned on cramming in as much as possible, as we wanted to feel like we were still living in luxury while in a small space. Our plan was to still feel like we were living our normal, daily lives, but just on a smaller scale. With more thought, however, we realized that not all of our must-haves were practical due to both size and weight of everything we wanted. We also realized that even though we were going to be in a small space, high ticket items would still add up. A high-end range and jetted

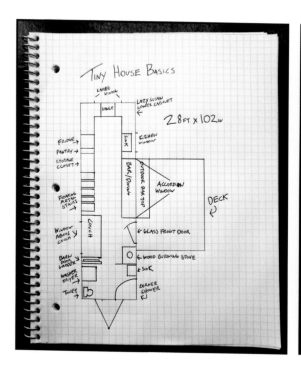

bathroom tub were still pricy, even though we were going to be in a smaller space. While the general construction will be far less expensive than a larger house, remember that high-end appliances will still add up fast. We also learned that just because we wanted more compact appliances vs. standard-sized appliances, that didn't mean they were necessarily going to be any cheaper. In fact, some things on a smaller scale can be more expensive than a standard size because they are less popular and need to be special ordered. We even thought about having our countertop depth be a little shorter in order to save space; however, we realized that we were again getting into custom sizing, which fetches a premium. Smaller doesn't always mean cheaper when it comes to appliances and custom finishes.

These are a few things to take into account, as well as researching beforehand if it's going to impact the size you are choosing for your tiny house. When we were planning our space, we accounted for at minimum apartment-sized appliances and standard-sized sinks and even shower inserts, as we knew we could readily get them without getting into custom pricing. If this were going to later change and we happened to find something in a different size, it wouldn't affect our space negatively. We recommend making must-haves lists. First "wish list:" all the dreamy things you would love to have in your home, from that sweet $7,000 Italian range to the most amazing hot tub to that solid glass wall that will slide to completely open up your space. Then make a list of things you need and use.

For example, if you love cooking or baking now, you will still love baking and/or cooking in a tiny house. Eliminating an oven and only having a stovetop, or going down to a two-burner range when you usually use three to four will get old.

Figuring out what you need for your lifestyle and daily habits will be key. For us, entertaining was still important in any space that we would be in. Since our home would only be 224 square feet on the bottom level, we knew we would need to design our house to utilize both the in and outdoors. Also, since we like to cook and entertain, having a good-sized kitchen to prepare for that was more important than storage of unused items.

However, storage was still very important, so we accounted for that as well. Since we are not minimalists, we also have lots of clothes and shoes that would need to be accounted for. For us, going tiny was more of a long-term solution, and we wanted to make sure all the amenities we were used to were accounted for. Of course, there would be some sacrificing; but we didn't want it to feel as though we gave up everything to make it happen. The key is in being balanced, which can be very hard in a small space. You don't want it all storage, to where the walls feel like they're closing in on you, but you also don't want to have SO many windows that they take over and don't allow for any storage. There is a way to have an open feeling with a good amount of windows as well as incorporating storage, which we will cover in the next chapters.

Ultimately, everyone's design is very personal and there is no one way to do it and no right or wrong. Design it how it makes YOU comfortable and you will be happy and content with it.

At that time, we were unable to see any actual tiny houses in person, so we decided to tape out the floor plan we had in mind. One of our many inspirations was the tiny house that Andrew and Gabriella Morrison built, which they call "hOMe." They had a lot of features we liked in a modern design, so we decided to tape out their floor plan on our driveway to give us a sense of size, which was 28 feet. This was very helpful in getting a sense of the size and space. While we decided to change a lot, the basics of the kitchen and bathroom being separated were still there. More importantly, it gave us a realistic way of seeing the size with our own eyes. One of the many things we remember about this process was that our soon-to-be tiny house would fit in our living room. We would come home and walk through the front door and count how many steps it would take to reach 28 feet. That was a scary thought indeed. We had never been in a tiny house and were going to build one purely on blind faith. All we could do at this time was hope we knew what we were getting ourselves into. After spending some time getting used to our awesome taped-out floor plan, we came to the decision that 28 feet in length would be the perfect fit for us. Yes, any extra foot added would bring more space to store our stuff, but we felt the length we chose was the perfect medium for moving when we needed and would not take up too much space at potential places to live. Now that we figured out the size we wanted to build, it was time to find a trailer to build on.

Buying Your Trailer

Once you've decided on the size for your tiny house, the next step is to buy your trailer. For us, this was a HUGE step. This was the commitment that we were actually doing this, we were going to build a tiny house! Our first purchase in this process was a washer/dryer combo, but come on, you can use a washer/dryer combo in any house, and really, it was not that big of a moment for us. Buying a trailer was a gigantic leap of faith into the tiny house journey; this was our turning point, there was no going back! Leading up to buying our trailer, we had lots of experience

with custom trailers in our past; we have had many custom trailers built for different lines of work over the previous ten years, and we have even built many custom trailers ourselves for different recreational pursuits. We were very confident in this process of designing our tiny house trailer; we were even confident that we could build the tiny house trailer ourselves with our background in welding and metal fabrication, but since we decided to do a large tiny house of 28 feet in length, we realized it would be quite difficult to manage large pieces of steel in the driveway of our rental house where we currently lived.

The decision was then made that we would have a manufacturer build our trailer for us to our specifications. The search started. We contacted every single trailer manufacturer and supplier on the western side of the United States, but we did not seem to get anywhere. Most trailer manufacturers hung up on us and said they didn't want anything to do with tiny houses, and others who supplied trailers for tiny houses wanted crazy amounts of money for the trailers. We felt like they were just trying to cash in, adding a "Tiny House Premium" to every trailer they quoted. It was as if we were throwing around the word "wedding" and getting a crazy premium for it being a niche item. We were shocked, but didn't give up. We kept calling and emailing everyone we could. We were just so surprised that even with the background we had in custom trailers and with the specifications that we provided, we still couldn't find anyone who was willing to work with us. There was a large disconnect between the needs for tiny houses and the manufacturers who built the trailers.

After more searching, we came in contact with a representative from a trailer factory that understood what we were trying to accomplish and who had experience with designing trailers. We felt relieved to find someone like Brad, our manufacturer representative, who understood our needs. We then worked with the manufacturer and designed a trailer that was perfect for the specific needs and load-bearing requirements of a tiny house foundation, and not just a modified utility trailer. Over the course of our tiny house build, we kept in close contact with Brad; he was very interested in the tiny house movement and curious to follow our journey as well. We talked regularly, discussing ideas for trailer designs and the features that would aid in better building practices for tiny houses. This sparked an idea in our head: if we had this much trouble locating a great source for a tiny house trailer with the background we had in regards to custom trailers, how many others were having this problem? This is when we realized that we can assist others in simplifying the process of going tiny by partnering with our representative and with the factory to provide custom tiny house trailers for others looking to downsize just like we were. By adding our experience we can help others better understand the ins and outs of the whole process of downsizing to a tiny house. This is how *Tiny House Basics* and our website www.TinyHouseBasics.com began.

Buying A New Trailer Versus A Used Trailer

Buying a used trailer is a perfectly good option, but there are many factors to consider. Has the trailer ever been overloaded? That is something you can't always determine by talking to the seller or by first glance at the trailer. Sometimes the problem rears its ugly head during its service life under your ownership. A couple things to look for include rust on the underside, and worn out components like bent axles, cross members, or framing. The plus side is you can sometimes get deals on used trailers, but it can come with a price later in the form of catastrophic failure. Over the course of a decade, we have had many custom trailers for all different lines of work, and one important thing I have learned is that most trailers "don't owe you anything after a few years." This means that the trailer was a usable item, and most trailers are overloaded and heavily abused during their service life, so five to ten years down the road, all the money spent on the trailer has really been accounted for. We have had many trailers that we have sold cheap in classified ads because they had rough lives with well-

worn components. With all the abuse I have personally put some of my old trailers through, I knew without a doubt that we would never build our tiny house on a used trailer; it was just too much risk, and there was no way to guarantee what happened to it throughout its life. I couldn't imagine spending all our savings on our tiny house and then trying to save a few bucks on the most important part of the build, the foundation.

When buying a new trailer, you can go to a trailer dealer and just buy one off the lot. Most trailer dealers will stock dozens of trailers to choose from. But these trailers will not be designed for a tiny house and for what you need in your build; you will end up still needing to modify a utility trailer build. These trailers will also not have an optimized design to handle the very specific loads of a tiny house structure. Trailer dealers, just like car dealerships, still have large mark-ups on every trailer, so chances are you will be paying top dollar for a trailer that still is not designed for a tiny house.

Every year we build hundreds of Tiny House Trailers for our customers, and each one is different. It is very rare that we build the same trailer, because everyone's needs are different. Do not settle for something just because it's on the lot or the builder has a size close to what you want. You will, after all, be living in this space; don't you think getting it built to suit your needs is the best thing to do for you and your family?

The last option we will mention is ordering a custom Tiny House trailer through us. From the beginning stages of our tiny house journey, we learned how to get the perfect trailer, and passed on that solution to many others looking to downsize. We learned to provide manufacturer direct pricing for all sizes of tiny house trailers and really understand the needs of our customers since we went through this whole process ourselves.

Yes, there are many tiny house trailer builders out there; many have a few designs tailored for a narrow base tiny house, and others make lavish claims about how great they are. No matter who you choose, do your research on the people behind the companies. There are a lot of startups without a proven track record just trying to cash in on the genuine movement. Like many of our customers, we are in it for the long haul; this is a lifestyle choice we made to simplify our lives, and what we are offering is our tiny house experience. We thoroughly researched every option for trailers out there, and I even posed the question to every owner behind every company: "Have you ever stayed the night in a Tiny House?" The answer shocked me—it was NO! How could they know what we needed if they never took a step in our shoes? That is why we carved our own way and teamed up with tried-and-true manufacturers that have been building for over thirty years to design our tiny house trailers. Every night we rest our heads under the roof of our tiny house. All the insight we have learned throughout the several years we have been living in our tiny house, we pass along to our people, our Tiny House People. That is the whole goal for us at *Tiny House Basics*: to simplify the process of going tiny, not complicate it. We build our tiny house trailers exactly for the needs of your build, and leave out anything you don't need.

CHAPTER 3

Downsizing

DOWNSIZING for us really started when we put down the deposit on the trailer. It was go time, it was really happening at that point. We knew there was no going back and it was time to get busy. We slowly started selling off the easy stuff that we knew we would not need in a tiny house in order to come up with the money for the deposit, but now it was time to assess everything we owned—and we owned a lot of stuff. We started selling off larger items that we knew would be easier to sell; fortunately, we had an old classic Austin Mini Cooper to sell, as well as a Triumph Bonneville motorcycle.

We sold these first in our steps to downsizing for a couple of reasons. Downsizing was not only necessary because we needed to come up with money to fund our tiny house build, but to also address ourselves on a deeper scale: what we needed in life and shelter. The Mini Cooper we owned had been a big part of our life since we started dating, and we thoroughly enjoyed owning it and driving it, but it occupied this recreational space in our lives which was shared with other things, like our motorcycle.

We started to think practically and really assess what activities were most important to spend our time, energy, and resources on, and narrow it down to just a couple of things. We realized that one of our biggest hobbies and joys was off-roading with our Toyota 4Runner and our off-road trailer.

Since this had also been a tradition for both of us, and camping was something we both grew up doing, we knew that while it was hard at first to give up our excess toys, our main priority was simplifying our life in all its forms and choosing one or two main activities to make memories without over-cluttering our life with many things. Every material item we owned had a cost; not only a monetary cost, but a cost in regards to the time out of our life it required to maintain. We had to address everything we owned and determine if the time each item required was worth it. Most things we owned didn't make the cut, as we favored selling off the majority of our things for funding our tiny house build and decluttering our lives in order to focus more on the things that mattered.

To keep our motivation through the downsizing process, we needed to see the fruits of our labor, so right when we started selling off our stuff we grabbed a big glass jar and stuffed our money in it from every item we sold. This little action really helped us physically see that we were slowly attaining our goal. We really suggest doing the same; pick out a piggy bank or a jar to store the funds you collect from the sales of your stuff. After every item you sell, you will most likely count the new total of the funds you have towards your tiny dream, just like we did. It was exciting and kept us motivated throughout the process. We started selling by

listing the most obvious and easiest things to sell first, things we knew without a doubt would not fit in our tiny house. We started with all our furniture: our couches, our chairs, our desks, and all other décor.

Even though our tiny house was going to be on the larger side, there was no way any of that stuff was fitting in our little abode once it was built. After most of our furniture that we could part with was gone, we turned our attention to our clothes, which we had a lot of. Selling clothes, whether on eBay or Craigslist is a very difficult process for a few reasons. We had personal attachments to many of our clothes, even pieces we never even wear anymore; we also had "goal" clothes from a time when we felt they fit us much better than they currently did.

The reality is that if you don't wear it now or have not within the past few months, you won't be wearing it anytime soon (of course seasonal clothes would be exempt). We would think that we would just hold onto

pieces we liked until they fit us better, but that is never the case. If you ever come to a time when that piece of clothing DOES fit you better, why would you want to put on an old piece of clothing versus celebrating and getting something new?

This philosophy took a while to sink in, so we held onto clothes we didn't wear even after the tiny house was built. However, we realized that the best way to handle this was to donate or give the clothes to people in need. So in one fell swoop we seriously went through every single item of clothes and decided whether we would wear this today; and if we didn't, we packed it up and brought it down to our favorite thrift shop and donated it all. Many people suggested this to us in the beginning, but for us, every single penny counted in our build and it just wasn't feasible to donate everything we owned. We needed to raise the money for our tiny house build because no one else was going to do it for us. But looking back on the majority of the small items we owned that were in good shape and couldn't easily be sold, it was best for us to donate so the items could be used by someone since we didn't have a need for them anymore.

During this process, our motivation and enthusiasm was at an all-time high, so we kept downsizing and selling off our stuff. We had a deadline, too, one we had committed to when we placed the deposit on our trailer: a deadline of eight weeks to come up with enough cash to pay for the balance on our trailer by the time it was finished being built. When we first placed our deposit down, eight weeks seemed like forever, but once we started downsizing our belongings, it came very quickly, almost too quickly. By the time we hit that eight-week deadline, we achieved our goal: to completely pay for the tiny house trailer by the time it was ready. This was just the first of the big hurdles to come, but it was very fulfilling to pack up our truck and head to Redding, California to meet our shipper and take possession of our tiny house trailer.

Little did we know that more downsizing was yet to come; after all, we had a full tiny house construction project to fund.

At this point, our downsizing process started to change. After we had placed the deposit on our tiny house trailer, and shortly after we had started selling off large items, we were contacted by FYI Network's *Tiny House Nation*. The show was brand-new and they were looking for people who were in the process of planning or building their tiny house. We had heard about the show, and at that time were nervous about it since it appeared it could possibly make the process of finding land to film the show on that much harder. We later learned that that wasn't the case at all. After we watched a couple of episodes of *Tiny House Nation*, we thought it might be something of interest to try out, so we responded.

Tiny House Nation asked us to send them our story of why we were going tiny, so we did that. After that, they were interested to find out that we were a young couple living in the San Francisco Bay Area who enjoyed the fun things that San Francisco had to offer, including dressing up to go out, and loved going off-roading and getting dirty and sleeping in remote places that were hard to get to. Since our story was intriguing to them, we started the interview/casting process. Boy oh boy, was that a rough and emotionally draining road! As exciting as it was to possibly be cast on the TV show, it was equally frustrating. From the onset of the many Skype interviews with the company based on the East Coast, it felt like total limbo.

In the very beginning, we were told that we were about 90 percent a "go" for the show. That last 10 percent of figuring out whether we were on the show was one of the most headache-inducing times. We never got a clear answer until the end of the three months as to whether it was guaranteed to happen. This left our timeline very much in the air. We had to plan for both cases, three to four months before filming began, or sticking to our original timeline of roughly nine months to a year. This was one of the toughest times for us, being in limbo and trying to figure out the unknown. Though a stressful time, it was also helpful, as it fueled us to keep going and to be prepared for whatever would end up coming our way. This put us in a mind frame of "hope for the best and prepare for the worst." Regardless of the stress of the unknown during that process, being mentally prepared for things to not go as originally planned helped us keep a balanced mind frame without easily getting frustrated. For us, having this situation of being in limbo was helpful in keeping us on track with downsizing and making sure we were prepared for what we hoped would happen. Either way, we were ahead of schedule with getting rid of stuff. Having a motivating deadline kept us from procrastinating like we normally may have done.

In the three-month casting process, we were required to have the layout and design we wanted nailed down, as well as having our contractors lined up and being prepared to have our full budget ready to go in case we did get cast. It was very different than we ever thought it would be getting on a "reality" television show. Either way, it was an exciting opportunity. In these three months of going back and forth with the network, we kept selling what we could that was smaller, apart from our formerly mentioned car and motorcycle. Part of the required process for the show was that we weren't to get rid of everything, as they still needed to do their "paring-down" skit with us. That was challenging, as we couldn't just keep our chunky items too close to the end of the process, leaving us scrambling at the last minute to sell items, such as our dining table and bedroom furniture and bar and couch. We wanted to sell off as much as possible so we didn't have to store it.

Once we finally got cast for the show, it was go time. We managed to pre-sell items, such as the dining table and bar and bed set; however, some buyers weren't going to be so patient (the couch went bye-bye before the film crew showed up). Once we pinned down filming dates with the show, as the filming process would be about two solid weeks, most of the buyers for our furniture were okay with waiting until after filming, thankfully. One of the ways we got a better idea of the size of our tiny house that we were designing and what would fit in it was to use the taped-out layout we had in our driveway.

This really put into perspective what size we would be working with and helped prepare our minds for what we were working with. This was a nice little reality check. We quickly realized that items, such as our favorite nesting tables and our fold away bar that we thought was "small," just wouldn't fit or be practical for a tiny house. We would regularly go out to our driveway floor plan and place chairs and try to imagine the walls and what space we had or didn't have. This little exercise helped us to get rid of more and more stuff much faster. We had also had little markers in the living room of our house as we walked in that helped us mentally prepare what size space we were working with, since we weren't going to be able to see a tiny house in person before moving into one. This helped us

understand how many steps it would take to walk across the entire length of what our tiny house would be, as opposed to what we were used to on a daily basis. The purge continued up until the film crew got there.

We managed to eliminate about 75 percent of our possessions by the time *Tiny House Nation*'s film crew arrived, which was four months from when we started purging. A funny thing starts to happen when going through your stuff and thinking about parting ways: you start to suddenly think you're going to use everything, and somehow suddenly everything has an emotional attachment to it. We remember this happening through the entire process: "Wait, wait, don't throw that one out, do you know how much that cost?!" Or, "I'm pretty sure that massive cabinet will somehow fit in the tiny house! Let's hold onto it just in case."

When it boiled down to getting rid of things, it proved to be a much bigger challenge mentally than we thought it would be. Since our downsizing process got cut much shorter than we had originally planned by being cast on the show, it really put pressure on us to try and be practical in our thinking about what we needed on top of ironing out the details of the design to be done well before the crews showed up. Unfortunately, with all the pressures of dealing with a television show, our purging came to a halt, and in the end we put about 25 percent of our items in storage. A lot of these items were personal things that we either wanted to give to family or friends, or some items that we just needed to disconnect emotionally from. It proved to be harder than we had expected to detach.

Fast forward a year after having stuff in storage and us ignoring it. We realized that the things that we thought were so important to us were things we couldn't even name anymore. We tried thinking long and hard about what we had in the storage unit that we were paying for every month. When we finally came to terms with the fact that we were completely content without these items, we were happy to get in there and get them sold or donated. While we don't suggest keeping a storage unit if you don't have to—it is MUCH easier to get rid of stuff beforehand—it did help us detach mentally and emotionally from it by having that time away from our stuff. One big and obvious downside to storing items that you likely don't need or won't use is that you will have to pay to store those things that you want to put off of having to deal with. We did end up making the money back, plus some, from the items we sold in our storage unit, but it would have been nicer to have been able to pocket that instead. After going through downsizing, we wish we would have been more brutally honest with ourselves in the beginning and had just gotten rid of mostly everything we truly knew wasn't going to fit, or things we used every once in a great while. That decision will have to be made at one point or another in your process of downsizing, and deciding to not deal with it and keep it out of sight might sound easier at the time, but it's tough either way. Looking back now and trying to remember what was even in that storage unit is pretty

much impossible. Once those items are gone, it's an unbelievably freeing feeling. It was amazing how we even slept better once we knew we didn't have that hanging over our heads anymore. From that experience, we have learned to regularly purge before letting things hang around for too long and letting ourselves get overly attached to a random item we purchased that never had any meaning to begin with. Hearing the saying "less is more" and now living that lifestyle, we truly see the benefits and feel the peace of mind that comes with it.

Tips For Downsizing

- Have you worn this item of clothing in the past month or the last season? If not, would you put it on now and go out in it? If the answer is again no, get rid of it.
- It is much easier to donate clothes than to try to resell; selling clothes is very laborious and time-consuming. It is great to donate to a good cause or someone you know in need.
- Avoid putting anything in storage if you can; you will have to address what is in there at some point in time, but procrastination will cost you lots of money in the meantime.
- Be realistic; will this item REALLY fit in your tiny house or new living arrangement?
- You do not have to be a minimalist to downsize. Be practical about what you need for your day-to-day lives.
- It's easier to give things away to friends and family if you have a hard time emotionally separating from certain material things.
- Do you need lots of different hobbies? Maybe think about focusing on a few of your favorites and downsize the others.

CHAPTER 4

Building: The Unspoken Realities Of Doing It Yourself, Plus The Cost

AFTER TAKING THE STEP in making the decision to downsize and now knowing that the first place to get the ball rolling is to start with the trailer, it's now time to figure out whether you want to take on building it yourself or whether you want to hire a builder to construct your tiny house. When we started our process, as we mentioned earlier, we watched as many YouTube videos as we could and thought we got a good sense of what it would take to self-build and what cost it would be to do it ourselves. We wanted our tiny house to be 28 feet long. For this size, we kept seeing a number of around $35,000, and only a few months to build it ourselves. Awesome, sign us up for that! That's cheaper than some cars. Who cares that we've never built a house or even a small shed, for that price we'll make it work. How hard can it really be? It is tiny after all. Oh, if only it was going to be that easy....

The Story Of How We Realized What Tiny Houses Actually Cost And How Easy Or Hard They Are To Construct

Before we went into contract with *Tiny House Nation,* and even before we started talking to them, we were gathering as much information as possible on all that would go into constructing the tiny house and roughly what the budget was going to be. When watching the many videos of some who used reclaimed materials or others who were already professional builders or contractors, we realized it was difficult to understand where their money was being applied. We never saw clear answers. Were the funds going towards building materials mainly, or all the finishing touches? What was the bulk of our budget going to go towards? If people were finding reclaimed materials, where were they finding them? Finding reclaimed materials in the San Francisco Bay Area was a challenge since they were very much in demand. Also, were these reclaimed materials going to be sturdy enough to assure the structural integrity of our house? How much time and effort was going to go into making these materials safe to work with? Is it better or even ok to build the main structure from reclaimed materials, or should it be new lumber?

We had SO many questions and so few answers to turn to. It was on us to find out. With the idea of materials aside, what about the tools we needed to build the house? We already had a large inventory of tools, but these were more related to metalworking and mechanic's tools, not woodworking, so we would need to start from scratch in that area, too. Assembling the appropriate tools for the job can cost thousands alone; yes, we could always rent the tools needed, but that could also add up quickly, too. Then there is the problem of location for the tiny house. Would we have to rent a spot, or could we find a friend or family that has land that would be open to an ongoing construction project? All these things must be factored into the whole budget of the house, and if they are not considered, they can end up being hidden expenses during the process of the build. So how do you decide what's the right approach for you and your circumstances? We're going to break down four different categories and the pros and cons of each to help you decide what would be the best route for you.

Building With A TV Show

When we first were contacted by *Tiny House Nation*, we were both excited and nervous as we had no idea what it would entail. We also weren't too thrilled about being on a show and being filmed during what we were assuming was going to be a stressful project. We were, however, curious to know if and what perks were involved with being on a TV show. With so many tiny house TV shows now, it seems more and more that people are documenting their build on a TV show.

When going through the interview process, one of the main things that appealed to us was the shorter timeline that was proposed. We were told to expect one week for the complete build and then we could move in. That was music to the ears of a couple who didn't have much woodworking and building experience. While we were excited to get started on our first self-build, we were also overwhelmed with the thought. Here are some pros and cons to help decide if building with a TV show is for you:

Pros:
- You'll get to assemble a large wish list for your tiny house, which is fun.
- The build time will be much less than you would be able to expect doing the job on your own.
- They will work with the budget that was agreed upon.
- They try their best to give you everything on your wish list, within reason; we did get a good amount from our list.
- They also try to nail down your design, incorporating your dream Pinterest desires and your design sketches.
- The crews are a lot of fun to work with, remaining light-hearted and making a stressful and unfamiliar process fun.
- The crew does a good job of making you feel special throughout the filming process; it's a little like it's your wedding day again and everyone is there to accommodate you.
- The reveal day for us was ACTUALLY a surprise and exciting.
- It's likely a once-in-a-lifetime experience that you won't be able to repeat.

Cons:
- The interview and qualifying process is long, and it can be frustrating to be in limbo for several months.
- You'll need to have your design and layout pinned down with rough drawings sent before getting cast on the show.
- The show does take credit for your design as its own; the 8-foot accordion/bi-fold window was our original plan along with the layout.
- You need to have your budget for the build ready to go as soon as you are accepted for the TV show.
- You're discouraged from getting rid of too much stuff before the show which can be tough when you need the funds from selling the items. We did the best we could, but had to sell a lot of larger items beforehand.

- You won't have complete control over where the funds are allocated to the build, which can leave you with things you don't want.
- The builds can actually take a couple weeks or longer, and it surely won't be done to completion. It will just look good for the cameras, and you will be left to do the finishing work, such as plumbing and connecting appliances, including the toilet and shower and even the wood stove, to get it to a livable state. It's basically a nice-looking doll house when they leave.
- They don't want all the tiny houses to look the same, so if you want to get on the show you'll need to have a "gimmick" of some sort to set

you apart from the others applying. Thankfully, ours was that sweet accordion window that we had wanted all along.

- If you're not used to being in front of a camera (and really who is), it feels very strange and makes it tough to really be yourself without feeling forced and cheesy. The filming days are long and exhausting.
- There is fake drama created out of small situations.
- Things went wrong on the build when outside contractors were brought in after our contractors had to return to other jobs after a week on the build.
- We're still fixing some things in our house from outside contractors who took advantage of it being a TV show and treated our house like a prop versus a home.
- You will likely have to micromanage what's happening on the build, which is annoying on both sides. If you don't, again, you will probably get something other than what you originally wanted.
- The cost of the build is misleading and is way lower than the actual cost, which can hinder anyone wanting to sell their tiny house in the future because they have likely invested a greater amount of money than what was stated on the TV show.
- It is a complete whirlwind and you won't know what's happening one day to the next. Patience and going with the flow will be key, otherwise you will be frustrated.

Building From The Trailer Up

Now for the majority of people, getting cast on a TV show is a far cry from reality, and most people will pursue one of the following three options we will discuss: building from the trailer up, having a shell built, or having the full build done for you. In retrospect, these options are far less complicated and less expensive than being involved with a TV network and the problems it adds to your tiny house build; after all, you want to simplify, not complicate, your life, right? Well, we will start from the foundation of the trailer and go from there. Building from scratch is the most involved but the most rewarding of options available. No matter the challenges that lie ahead, the feeling of accomplishment cannot be compared to anything else. The biggest advantage of doing the complete

build yourself is you can go at your own pace and not stray too far from your budget. You can truly pay as you go, which is an option that is not as available in the other options we will discuss. You will also learn by doing, which we feel is one of the best ways to learn any skill. You can read up on the skills you need to build a house, but putting those skills into practice is the rewarding experience. You will make mistakes—you will make lots of them—but that is the beauty of learning, and these mistakes, no matter how costly they may be in wasted materials, will never be forgotten, and you can pass on the things you have learned to other people looking to go down the same path you chose to simplify your life. Here are the pros and cons of building from scratch:

Pros:

- The build moves at your own pace.
- The ability to control your budget by saving money on labor.
- Learning the skills needed for building, which you can apply to future projects.
- Satisfaction of building your house from the foundation to the finish.
- The added time it takes for the build can work to your benefit so you have more time to interact with the space and make needed

adjustments in the design along the way (we changed many aspects of our design during the building process).

- Ability to use reclaimed materials (new lumber is always recommended for framing and sheathing of the house).

Cons:

- Must remain self-motivated to keep the progress going.
- Time-involving; most people work, and therefore adding a tiny house construction project into the mix can delay the projected completion timeline for the build.
- If it is your first construction project, you will need to factor in the time to learn how to build and use the tools properly.
- Extra money needed to buy the tools required to build if you do not own them already.
- Resale value: when it comes to selling your tiny house (if you ever do), you will not get as much back as you would if the whole project had been built by a licensed contractor, but the money you save on living expenses overall will overshadow the loss in resale.
- Finding a place to build the tiny house.

Starting With A Shell And Building To Completion

What does a shell typically consist of? The shells we build for our customers included one of our tiny house trailers, 2x4 construction, vapor wrap, windows, front door, standing seam metal roof with a style of your choice, and siding. There are limitless options, like custom windows and adding electrical and plumbing.

The Tiny House movement should be about affordability and a high-quality end product. Many people just like us are looking for more affordable options for housing, and that is why many of us choose to build our own tiny house with our own hands on a tiny scale. But what if you are overwhelmed by the actual construction of your tiny house and you do not feel you have the skills to take care of the heavy labor part of framing? One growing popular option is to have the shell of the house professionally built by a contractor, and you can then finish the interior yourself. This is a great way to ensure you have a properly built house but

one that also saves a lot of labor on the finished product. Many people are drawn to building tiny houses because of the DIY nature of building their own home. Having the structure done in part by a professional still retains the spirit of DIY but with the heavy lifting alleviated. This path will help save a lot of money in the long run. For both of us, a lot of the fun when designing our tiny house came from designing the interior to fit our needs and desires. (We will talk more about our design in the next chapter.) We did do our build from the trailer up like discussed earlier, but if we did it all over again, we would have gone for the shell route; it would have saved a lot of time but still given us the satisfaction of finishing the house ourselves. After all, we still had lots of repairs and changes after the crew of *Tiny House Nation* left; it was pretty much like a shell anyway since nothing worked! The pros and cons of starting with a shell include:

Pros:

- Professionally-built structure
- The hardest part of building, the framing, is done for you
- More resale value
- Still retains the DIY spirit
- Much more affordable that having the whole tiny house built for you
- Speeds up the build time
- Finding a place to finish the tiny house will be easier as a shell, since it will not appear to be a full construction project

Cons:

- Cost: paying for professional labor to build the structure will eat into your budget
- Fast timeline may prevent the pay-as-you-go method
- Not having the satisfaction of building every part of the house yourself

Having The Complete Build Done For You

With tiny house builders popping up all over the country, it is easy to see the movement is growing and the ability to find a reputable contractor to build your tiny house is getting easier. Hiring a contractor to completely build your tiny house just for you is the easiest option available, but this easy option does come with a large price tag. Most custom tiny house builders charge from $35,000 for small 18 foot tiny houses up to well past $100,000 for the custom-style ones you have likely seen on TV.

One of the biggest downsides we have seen with ordering a complete tiny house through a builder is space planning and practical design. There are virtually no builders out there who actually live in a tiny house, so there is a major disconnect with space planning. We have yet to meet a builder or owner of a tiny house company that has ever slept a night in one of their tiny houses. Many builders may feel they understand what the customer wants in their design, and it may look great on the boards of Pinterest, but so many custom tiny houses we see lack practical space planning for long-term living in a tiny house. Sometimes we joke that the real reasons we see tiny houses built on TV shows pop up for sale almost immediately after the show airs are due purely to poor space planning and layout. The pros and cons of having the complete build done for you include:

Pros:
- Fastest option to a move-in ready tiny house
- Experienced builder and designer to help guide you through the process

Cons:
- Highest cost option
- Cost of shipping if you use an out-of-state builder
- The design the builder has in mind may not translate into practical use of interior space.
- The research involved in finding a reputable builder

A Few Things To Think About And Take Into Consideration

Regardless of what route you decide to go with, some of the major things to keep in mind will be: if building yourself, where will you build? When we were looking for land, one of the things we found was that some people were willing to rent us land to live on, but not to build on. Many did not want to deal with construction going on at their property, even if it was tiny. This was completely understandable; the timeline for construction of the average self-built tiny house seems to be ranging around a year, sometimes longer. While searching and hunting for reclaimed materials is like an exciting treasure hunt, one must factor in the time involved to find such materials. We have seen countless YouTube videos of tiny house builds stating the person has built their house for only a few thousand dollars using reclaimed materials, but the truth of the matter is they never brag about how many countless hours they spend hunting and searching for those free materials. The adage "time is money" is very true in this situation, and you need to factor in how much your time is worth to you. The best option will depend on your own set of circumstances and building skill level. There will be a trade-off in any situation; either you'll save time or you'll save money. For some, time is money, and for others, it's more important to learn or sharpen a skill through this process. Whichever direction you decide to choose, just remember to be realistic in how much time you have to dedicate to the project. Being honest with yourself, and even being realistic about your skill level, will be helpful in keeping the process going smoothly. Making your own pros and cons list can be helpful by having points and reminders to reference when deciding which route to go. There is no right or wrong way to tackle building or having a tiny house built as long as it works for you.

CHAPTER 5

Why We Chose Our Design Aesthetic And Layout

PLAYING WITH AND FIGURING OUT our layout and design was one of the most enjoyable parts of planning. This is where imaginations really get to run free. We had visions of all our furniture being convertible and multipurpose, while being art pieces at the same time. We wanted custom everything. Given that it was going to be a tiny house, we naïvely felt that we would be able to afford custom everything on a small scale, right? We'll talk more in depth on this throughout this chapter. To get going on our overall design, we needed to start with the first and most important step, the layout and the exterior of the house. Since we ended up getting cast for a TV show, our time to nail down the layout and design had become extremely limited. We had to get serious quickly about what we had in mind. Some know exactly what they want instantly and never look back or second-guess themselves; that, however, was not our case.

As you embark on your tiny house dreams, don't let the fear and uncertainty bring you down. We changed our minds daily during this time. Since we had never even set foot into a tiny house or even seen anything remotely like one in person, we were in unchartered waters. Did it scare us to try and figure how we were going to be investing our

precious savings in designing a very small home when we had never even set foot into one and weren't going to get the chance to? It sure did! It was hard for us to truly wrap our minds around how a bottom level of 224 square feet and a total of 374 square feet, including lofts, would be like to interact with on a daily basis, especially coming from a 1,300-square foot house with a two-car garage, FULL of gear and tools. So how were we going to figure out how to do this without setting foot into one to see how functional they are? How can we possibly even imagine what the size would be like when we live in something much larger than 374 square feet? The fun begins....

As we've mentioned in previous chapters, lots and lots of research is key. We looked at as many photos and videos as we possibly could; we were so deep in Pinterest and Instagram images it was ridiculous. Our boards kept growing to the point where it felt as though they were out of control. Our wish list also grew, and so did the price range of appliances and finishes that we now wanted. Oh, Pinterest. Since the $8,000 cute little Italian range we had our eye on wasn't attainable, it was time to peel ourselves away from the boards and dreaming, and time to start measuring for what we really could fit into the house and also afford. Since we were now on a time limit, we had to stop the dreaming and get real with our decisions.

The Exterior Look

The exterior is what draws the crowds. After all, look at it. It's a normal looking house, but tiny in size. These cute designs are what we feel has added to the huge popularity of the movement—the freedom to design your house exactly as you see fit. You can have a tiny little house with bright colors and whimsical trim, or you can have a big old box to maximize the space on the inside. It is the balance of maximizing space on the interior but also creating an appealing design on the exterior that can be the most challenging. If you look at most tiny houses with their steep pitched roof lines and extra small footprint, they all have a trade-off inside. With a steep roof pitch comes a closed-in loft for sleeping; with lack of windows comes a dark interior. These were all things we heavily weighed when considering our design. Taking inspiration from

many tiny houses we have seen in New Zealand and in the United States, we decided on the more modern shed or slant roof line. This would have one side of the house with a high wall and one side of the house with a low wall. This modern design would create more space inside of the tiny house, especially in the loft where we would sleep. Considering our moderate climate in Northern California, we wanted to have a very minimal pitch roof to allow the most interior space, but still enough slant to give the house character and provide proper runoff for rain in the rare case we got it.

For the exterior, we decided on a size of 28 feet. We chose 28 feet because to us, this seemed like a happy medium. With the movement ever growing, tiny houses are growing in size as well. Originally, they seemed to be right around 100-150 square feet or so. A king-sized bed is 42.15 square feet, so roughly two-and-a-half king-sized beds would make up a 100-square foot tiny house, not including lofts. This seemed impractical for us and our needs. On the other side of the spectrum, we're seeing more and more tiny houses going up to as large as 40 feet long, which would mean 340 square feet, not including any lofts. While a size such as 40 feet can be appealing to many, one of the main deterrents or drawbacks for most is the added cost and time to build it. So, we really thought about our budget and time frame, and after looking at many examples that were approximately 28 feet, we knew it was the most attainable for our budget, timeline, and what we wanted in a tiny house. Another factor we considered when choosing this size was its portability. We weren't planning on traveling with it; however, we did want to be able to move with ease if we did decide to move. We also took into consideration our hilly terrain—lots of trees— and towing a tiny house in addition to the length of a truck around tight corners and steep driveways. We are thankful that we considered these factors, as our land happens to be steep and narrow with lots of trees and a tight turn. One of the final deciding factors was that we didn't have any near-future plans to buy land, which meant we would be renting land. We wanted a size that was still very comfortable but wouldn't feel overly large so it would be appealing to any potential landlords. We considered 28 feet to be a modest yet practical and comfortable size. A 28-foot tiny house, 8 1/2 feet wide would give us 224 square feet on the bottom floor of the interior space; it would be comparable to a one car garage. Our added lofts, one 7 feet deep and one 12 feet deep, would give us an extra 150 square feet of interior space. So think a one car garage with a nice large storage attic above it.

What Size Tiny House Should You Build?

Everyone's needs are different, so that would require some self-reflection on your part to decide which size would fit you best. Our custom tiny house trailers are available in any size, from 10 feet to well above 40 feet long. We can build to suit almost anyone's needs. Below are some common sizes and what they are best suited for to help you determine if that size would be appropriate for you.

14-feet tiny houses are commonly built with a single loft and are very travel-friendly. The tiny house built on them can be lightweight, so that most full-size pickups can tow them with ease. This size tiny house trailer can accommodate a small kitchenette, toilet, and bedroom with very thoughtful planning. These trailers are most commonly ordered in 10k to 12k GVWR (gross vehicle weight rating)

20-feet tiny houses are very popular for single people and sometimes couples with good space planning. This size tiny house trailer is most commonly built with one sleeping loft and one small storage loft, a small kitchenette, and bathroom with shower. These trailers are most commonly ordered in 10k to 12k GVWR.

24-feet tiny houses are one of the most popular sizes for couples who plan to travel often. There is a vast number of designs and floor plans available for this size tiny house. The 24-foot length still provides an open living space and maneuverability when towing. This size tiny house trailer provides room for a nice-sized kitchen, larger lofts, and larger bathroom for a spacious floor plan. These trailers are most commonly ordered in 12k, 14k, and 15k triple axle GVWR.

28-feet tiny houses are the most popular sized we build trailers for. This size also has a special place in our hearts, as we built our own tiny house on one of these trailers. This is an extremely comfortable size for a tiny house. This size tiny house trailer provides enough room for a full kitchen, full bathroom, two larger lofts, and an open, spacious feeling. These trailers are most commonly ordered in triple axle 18k and 21k GVWR.

30-feet and above tiny houses: These sized tiny houses can be outfitted with all the creature comforts you can think of, like a very large kitchen, larger bathroom, and even larger lofts on both sides. Tiny houses longer than 30 feet are very popular for families of all sizes. This length allows large lofts that can be closed off to create separate spaces for children and parents. These trailers are most commonly ordered in triple axle 21k GVWR.

The Kitchen

The kitchen is the heart of most houses where everyone gathers. Our kitchen in our previous house was a decent size in square footage, but it was lacking in many ways. Since that kitchen wasn't designed by us or for us, we quickly figured out what we disliked. When we were planning for our own design for the tiny house kitchen, we wanted to make it fit our needs even in a small space. One of the main things we knew we wanted in our layout of the house was the kitchen and bathroom on separate ends of the house. For starters, we wanted the kitchen to be a decent size, so having it on its own end would allow that, but we didn't want to have to deal with people walking through the kitchen to get to the bathroom. Since we had planned on entertaining often, having people walk through the kitchen while we were cooking and making cocktails would get frustrating and possibly dangerous, as we are all over the place in the kitchen. Also, we thought about how it would be for us going to someone else's house when we had to use the restroom and knowing they were just standing right on the other side of the door...preparing food. That could be awkward.

With us being a couple who enjoy entertaining while cooking and making cocktails and getting very messy while in the process, a good-sized kitchen with ample countertop space was a priority. Our kitchen now fits the two of us very comfortably so we can both get in our zones without getting in each other's way. We actually have more countertop space in our tiny house than we had in our previous house and we love it. Since we were going to have the kitchen on one end, we went with a U shape because we did want it to be a nice size. This shape allowed for us to have both ample countertop space along with normal amenities, such as a large double basin sink. We went with a large sink because we do use our kitchen a lot and we were going to forego a dishwasher to allow more lower cabinet storage space. Has living without a dishwasher been an adjustment? Sure, at times it's not a big deal as long as we're consistent and keep on top of doing dishes right away. For those times when we fail to do the dishes right away, we miss having a dishwasher. We have considered installing a smaller drawer style dishwasher under the sink at some point. Until then, having a big sink has been extremely helpful, and

has been one of our favorite things about the kitchen. We started to see a trend in tiny houses that had cute small kitchens, and even smaller sinks. This was a turnoff for us, since a little detail such as a small sink didn't seem practical long-term. It would have been a frustrating thing to deal with, since we use our kitchen and its dishes often. We knew we didn't want to have an argument daily about who was doing dishes, knowing that we would hate every second of it trying to work with a tiny sink. Doing dishes is already not fun, no need to make it even more difficult with an unusually small sink. Go with the size that will be comfortable long-term for you.

We opted for a 24 inch apartment sized range versus the standard 30 inch model because it was still plenty large, with four burners and ample oven space which stores most bakeware when not in use. We weren't willing to give up an oven for lower cabinet space. We enjoy using the oven as much as we do the range top. We always encourage people to keep in mind when going tiny you don't have to give up everything you enjoy and are used to just because you're downsizing. If you enjoy roasting in your oven or baking, you will still enjoy it in a tiny house. We have zero regrets with having both an oven and range top.

We also have a 10.2 cubic foot apartment-sized refrigerator. This has proved to be plenty of storage for the two of us. It prevents food waste, something we were guilty of regularly when we had a larger 22 cubic foot fridge in our previous house. Since this was going to be our first time in a smaller space, we did leave room around the refrigerator in case we felt we needed a larger one. So far, we've been happy with the apartment-sized one, and have found it fits our needs. We enjoy a mix of eating at home and eating out. If you're one who makes all meals at home, 10 cubic feet may not be as feasible. Next to the refrigerator we have a slim pull-out pantry cart for our dry food storage. When we were working on downsizing, we had a good-sized pantry. However, we learned that the majority of that dry food often expired or got pushed back so far behind other dry foods that we never knew they were there, leading to more food waste. So this size of a small pull-out pantry has been sufficient, and allows us to actually see what we have on hand.

The cabinet next to the refrigerator and dry food storage is our utility closet. This closet, for us, never originally had a specific purpose, other than the circuit breaker panel and basically our catch-all area. It's one area that was never completely finished inside, as we never intended it be an attractive show piece. It basically holds our junk. It wasn't well designed with a nice finish, although that is in large part because the TV show just threw it together. We always thought we would finish it out or redesign it nicely, but it's honestly low on our to-do list as it still functions and holds our stuff. Some of the main items that stay in there are a foldable ironing board and iron, along with a small clothes steamer and a little vacuum cleaner and office supplies. We also added an atmospheric water generator from Outpost Eco to the cabinet. It creates drinking water from the humidity in the air, which it then filters with an alkaline filter. The unit both heats and cools the water. With California being prone to drought

conditions, it's been nice knowing we're simply using the humidity in the air and are having good clean water to drink from it.

Moving on to our upper shelving for plates and cups, we opted for open shelving so it would give the feeling of open space. This does mean we have to be more mindful of keeping it organized, but it's been easy to do. It also helps us realize if and/or what we do use on a regular basis, which helps us get rid of what we don't need. Since one of us has a bit of a glassware buying problem, the open shelving is a nice reminder that we can't simply cram more in without it looking cluttered. Plus, the easy access for us to both put dishes away and grab them off the shelf is an added bonus that we've learned to appreciate. It's the little things. Across from the open shelving we have our little barware area displayed on a decorative metal shelf, as well as decanters next to it for nicer spirits and a wine rack above.

For our lower cabinet space, we have space under the sink with drawers on each side of the sink. Across from the sink there are two full lower cabinets, with two slim drawers above it and another small pull-out pantry area on one side of the range. Then on the other side of the stove in the corner, we have a Lazy Susan, which holds a ton of stuff. We find that it's actually more space than we thought we originally needed, and because of this, we were able to bring all of our favorite and often-used larger kitchen tools, such as:

- Vitamix
- Juicer
- KitchenAid mixer
- Food processor
- Crockpot
- Several coffee vessels

These were items we had invested in and used often, so we were not willing to give up those creature comforts just because we were downsizing. In our layout and design, we wanted to make sure to account for the things we needed and used regularly. There were some inexpensive items that we didn't use often at all and felt ok with selling or donating; if we felt we needed them down the line we could purchase them at that

time. So far, we have not had to do that, as we very carefully analyzed what we were actually using when downsizing as opposed to what we liked to keep around just in case. Being practical both in getting rid of things that are hardly ever used but also in making space for the things you love and have invested in will result in a more comfortable long-term tiny house living situation.

The Accordion Window / Bar Area

The 8-foot accordion window is by far our favorite feature of our home. We really wanted an open feeling in our house with as many windows as possible to let in natural light. When we were thinking of a dining situation, we originally had several ideas for furniture that would be convertible. After redesigning what our convertible dining table and seats would look like, we realized that for us, having to convert and move our stuff around daily would get old fast. Don't get us wrong, there are some great pieces

of convertible furniture out there that are well designed, but for us and our needs, it just wasn't practical. We needed a space that can be easily accessible and hassle-free. The accordion window was something we saw on Pinterest, generally in large kitchens, that was above sinks and countertops. We knew that would be a perfect fit for what we wanted to have as a main feature in our home. Once we stumbled upon it we were hooked—we knew we needed to have one and to design our space around it. This space for us is multifunctional, without our having to move anything around or convert the space. It's our dining table for meals, and also our computer work space. With the accordion window open and the exterior countertop on the other side of the window, it becomes dining for six to eight people. Having the window open out onto the deck allows it to be even more of a social space that allows for more people being able to gather, while still having a place to sit and set drinks down and lean on while enjoying being outside. For us, the accordion window over the interior and exterior countertops is the perfect solution for work, entertaining, and

a space to enjoy meals. Below the window and countertop is the covered wheel well. We use it as a footrest.

Stairs & Ladders

When designing a tiny house, many people have to decide if they want stairs or a ladder leading up to their lofts. For us, a ladder to our main loft was just not practical for the long-term. We always planned to do stairs, but what kind of stairs? Most people want to maximize the storage space in their home, but that comes at a price: a closed-in feeling in the already narrow footprint of an 8-foot wide tiny house. So what compromise would we come up with? We decided to have one set of stairs for the main loft, and a ladder for the second loft. For the stairs, we wanted to create a visual pass through them, and we were not too concerned about storage built into the stairs. While searching through Pinterest, we came across a metal staircase used in a small dwelling in New Zealand, and this is where we developed our idea. To improve on this concept, we designed the stairs to float off the wall with each step as a single wall mounted landing with a handrail to connect several of the stairs to the landing in the loft. Each stair was built with a quarter-inch steel plate and one-and-a-half-inch Drawn Over Mandrel steel tubing with the help of our very good friend and fellow welder Ray. He fabricated the stairs for us and the stair tread was done by one of the carpenters from *Tiny House Nation* in a beautiful Epay and Oak mix. With a limited footprint for the stairs, we decided to skip the last step that would rise into the loft, and therefore encourage users to kneel into the loft from that last floating stair. With this design of the stairs floating off the wall, you could visually see through the stairs, and this added to a feeling of spaciousness. Yes, we did lose a storage option that could have possibly been built into the stairs, but the compromise was worth it. We later added some small cubbies that followed the steps of the stairs and created some storage. This is one of those matters that is definitely personal preference, as floating stairs with exposed storage may not be ideal for some or fit their lifestyle and needs. At times, it can be an effort to keep the area tidy and to remember to not let it become our catch-all. Even so, for us the tradeoff was worth it in order to have a more open feeling. This is a good time to really think about your daily needs and even take inventory of your items that will be going with you in order to know whether you can do something similar, and if the effort of keeping it from being a messy eyesore will be worth it to you or not. Storage stairs are a great way to hold a lot of items and a good way to keep the stuff inside covered with little doors if need be.

The entrance to the second closet loft on the other side of the tiny house required a further compromise. It was not reasonable to have a second set of stairs; we would have had to forgo a living room couch, and that was not going to happen. The original plan was to have a wall-mounted ladder to climb to the loft next to the sliding door for the bathroom, but during the framing portion of the tiny house build we scratched that plan because a door sliding to the opposite wall would get in the way of the wood burning stove we had planned. We decided to just put the ladder on the door and give it a dual purpose. We purchased a heavy-duty sliding barn door kit, installed a heavy solid core door, and used three-quarter-inch black pipes for the ladder rungs. Underneath the ladder rungs we used reclaimed oak to give the door more character. To make entry into the second loft easier, we built small half-walls or parapets on the sides, with handle grips to make getting into the second loft easier.

Bathroom

We desired a lot for our 42-square foot tiny house bathroom. We needed to fit in a washer/dryer combo, a toilet, a sink, and a huge shower. We pulled it off and the main reason was the addition of a full glass corner shower. This visual pass through of a full glass shower made the small 42-square feet space of the bathroom seem much larger than it actually is. Next to the shower, with 20 inches of space, we installed a narrow sink and vanity found at Ikea, and opposite the shower and sink we installed a composting toilet and a vent-less washer/dryer combo with corner shelving above for all our bathroom and laundry needs. Between the composting toilet and the corner shower, we have a large narrow window to create ventilation and light for the bathroom.

Living Room Area

Our living room area is 7 feet long and 8 feet wide. In the living area, we have a 72 inch apartment-sized couch that butts up against the stairs and wheel well on one side and the barn door ladder on the other. There is a large window above the couch, and across from it, a front door with a full glass window that allows for a lot of natural light and helps make the space feel larger and more open. The space also allows for an ottoman that we can roll out from under the stairs when we want to lounge and put our feet up. In our old house, we had a chaise longue sofa and thought that downsizing to a smaller sofa would be difficult, since this was the area that we were sacrificing to have more entertaining space. However, we have been very happy with the compromise. It's still very comfortable, and we both have plenty of space to stretch out on a comfortable sofa. While storage is important, we knew that we didn't want to sacrifice our movie watching comfort with a bench style couch that had storage in it, but rather wanted to make sure we had a real couch as we were planning on tiny living being a long-term solution. In order for that to be the case, we knew we couldn't sacrifice what felt both comfortable and normal to us, and we are SO glad we chose a normal feeling couch. In this living space, we also have a Kimberly wood burning stove for heat and ambiance. We were used to having a wood burning fireplace in our house before and absolutely loved it; we loved the warmth, the smell, and the ambiance. So we set out to look for one on a small scale. This small wood burning stove was made for small spaces and made to have minimal clearance behind it, making it ideal for a tiny house or even a boat. Above the wood burning stove, we have our 40 inch TV on a moveable wall mount roughly 3 feet above the stove. The question we get asked everyday in the colder months is, "Does the stove affect the TV?" The answer? "No." The wood burning stove mostly radiates heat from front, as designed. A little bit of heat comes from the top and almost no heat comes off of the back side. We do have our TV on a movable arm on the wall in case it does start to feel a little too warm. We haven't had any issues with the TV getting too warm.

In addition to the wood burning stove, we have a mini split system above the couch that produces both hot and cold air. In the area we live

in we can have temperature extremes. Having an A/C and heater was necessary. Since the mini split can be an energy hog, we try and use it as little as possible, mainly in the winter months. We've supplemented having to use our mini split in the winter with the wood burning stove, and in addition to that, we've added a small Envi wall mount heater behind our couch. It's a very low energy and low profile convection heater that keeps the tiny house at a comfortable temperature while we sleep and are away during the day. Since we work from home and tend to be in and out of the house throughout the day, it's not always practical for us to keep a fire going. Having this low profile and low cost unit was an ideal addition to keeping our little abode comfy.

Second Loft/Closet Space

Above the bathroom we have the second loft, and it's the smaller of the two which we use as a closet/vanity makeup area. This space is 7 feet deep by 8 inches wide, totaling 56 square feet. On one side of the loft we have hanging clothes for the entire depth of 7 feet; this is plenty of hanging clothes space for us since we were used to small closets in our last house. On the other side of the loft we have eight small drawers as our dresser space, storing some shoes and hats on top of them. In between the two clothes areas and below one of the windows is the vanity area. We chose to have the vanity area separate from the bathroom since it's what we were used to in our previous home, and liked how it worked as a separate space. We also have two windows in the loft, so it has nice cross-ventilation.

Master Loft

The main sleeping loft is the larger of the two and spans 100 square feet (the size of some smaller tiny homes), with stairs that lead to the loft to make it easier to get in and out. With the shed roof, we have a low side at 3 feet at the top of the stairs, and the high side is 3 feet 9 inches. With the "huge" size of this loft, we installed the same size bed we were used to in our old house, a king-sized bed. This size allowed us to have room on both sides of the bed and plenty of area between the foot of the bed and the stairs. To maximize storage in the loft and to create an open feeling, we raised the floor surrounding the bed and added cubbies to store our clothes and miscellaneous items. There are long storage cubbies that wrap around the bed for lesser-used items, including behind the headboard. Also around the bed we have three sliding windows for plenty of cross-ventilation and a large 40-inch wall-mounted TV on the high side of the loft. Yep, that's right, we have two TVs. in a 374-square foot house. Like a lot of people, we occasionally enjoy snuggling up in our cozy loft and watching TV in our bed. This was something we enjoyed in our previous house, and even though we decided to downsize, we knew that wouldn't change. With the floor storage raised up to surround the bed, it made it easier to get in and out of bed with both floor levels about the same height. We also installed FLOR carpet tiles on every floor cubby to make it that much easier on our knees when crawling into bed.

When designing and decorating, you can define any space and make it personalized so your space is unique to you. The little special touches in your design and décor will set your space apart from any other. Since tiny houses are, well...small, it will likely be small touches that keep your space fresh. Tiny houses are unconventional, and generally so are its owners. Gone will be the artistic restrictions of conventional landlords. Tiny houses are the perfect marriage for those craving to express themselves artistically by having the space they live in reflect what makes them happy.

We designed our home to meet our daily needs, and because we intend to live in it long-term, we made sure to add as many creature comforts as possible to keep us loving our space for many years to come. We can't stress it enough. Evaluate your own personal daily habits and needs and be practical with your design and space planning. For some, 20 feet may be too small, while for others, 38 feet is far too large and loses the tiny house feeling. We all have personal tastes and preferences, and that's what makes so many tiny houses great and unique like each of us. Regardless of what size you decide to choose, you can make your space as special and as comfortable as you want it.

CHAPTER 6

Making Room For Your Junk In A Small Space

WE ALL HAVE STUFF that we can't part with, whether they are items that are sentimental, functional, decorative, or even just stuff we like for no reason but know we don't want to give up. So when you decide to downsize and go tiny but want to own more than just a few items, how do you work storing items into your design without having the walls feel as though they're closing in on you? Is it really possible to downsize and be a non-minimalist in a tiny space? Can your space have functional and decorative pieces without it feeling cluttered? Yes it can, and we'll show you what's worked for us and what we've had to tweak over the years to make form and function work.

Interior Storage

When we were figuring out our layout and design, we knew we needed to account for as much storage as possible, but we also wanted it to feel as open as possible. As we've mentioned earlier, we never planned on being minimalists, but we also didn't want to live in a house of clutter. With a small space, storage and organization are always an ongoing puzzle. For

those who are naturally organized and are able to keep things in place, we are envious of your organized brains and downsizing will be quite a bit easier for you. For the rest of us...there is going to be some trial and error; ok, not some but LOTS of trial and error. We can't tell you how many times we thought something might work, and it did for a period of time, but inevitably it would fall apart. While having a place for every single item is the goal and the dream no matter what size home we have, it's generally not realistic for a lot of us. We love when we have a dedicated space for everything, but the reality is that sometimes we're running in and out of the house and simply don't have time to put items back in their special spots, even in a small space. So here are a few things that have and haven't worked for us over the years.

Storage Bins

We all love those storage bins, from the cute little cube ones to the wood crate style bins or metal bins. Storage bins are where it's at. What we love about storage bins of all types is that you can keep your items in them nicely organized or just throw a bunch of stuff in them and dig through when need be. We always start off with nicely organized storage bins, and then as time goes on, they become a jumbled mess—but that's ok, because either way the items aren't visible in them. Having your bins labeled is especially helpful, so if you do have to dig, at least you'll know which bin to dig in. It's kind of an organized chaos kind of situation. It'll also help you keep your own stuff where it needs to be if there's more than one person in the house and you have issues about taking over any possible empty spot of space that might not be yours for the taking. One of the main areas we've utilized storage bins in is the bathroom. We have eclectic taste and we originally had a bunch of mismatched bins, thinking it would work, but it didn't. Since we have them displayed on open shelving, it started to look messy and unorganized. When we finally found metal storage bins that we liked, we replaced them all and went with many in the same style to keep the look organized. Just because you want an organized, clean look doesn't mean you have to go with the most boring and neutral-colored items. We added small storage bins that were a brass color to give it some style and added a few larger bins that were a dark metal. Mixing the metals makes it more visually appealing, but it's not over-the-top or too bright for the small space.

Cubby Floor Storage

When we were on the TV show *Tiny House Nation*, one of the things that was actually designed by their team was the cubby floor storage, since they knew we had A LOT of clothes and had no intentions of giving them up. Despite what was seen on the show as our "pare down," we in fact did not get rid of most of those clothes during that time, as we were still wearing most of them. So with inspiration from Pinterest images we provided, they came up with the design of the cubby floor storage. For our master loft around our king-sized bed, we have three large floor storage cubbies, four medium-sized cubbies, and six small, long, skinny

cubbies around the actual bed. This storage has been great; it was originally designed to function as our in-floor dressers. While we did use it as just that for the first year or so, it ended up not being functional for us long-term as a dresser. In the time that we did use it as a dresser, it ended up holding as many clothes as a large six-to-eight-drawer dresser would. Some downfalls of using it for our clothes storage was, for one, it was on the opposite side of the tiny house where our hanging clothes were, so we had to climb up to two different lofts for clothes. In the beginning, it didn't seem as though it would be a problem, but after some time it did get old. Another reason it didn't work for our folded clothes was because dust and sometimes dirt seemed to settle between the cracks of the cubbies, which would then settle onto our clothes. We've moved our folded clothes to the other loft and now use these for general storage as well as shoes that rotate from season to season. Even though they didn't end up working for our clothes, the amount of storage they hold has been extremely helpful for many general items. Since these floor cubbies have been built up around our king-sized bed, it makes our bed appear as though it's mostly flush with the floor. One of the main things that we love about this is how clean it looks and how open it feels. It's nice that, again, even if it's not organized inside these floor storage cubbies, the space still appears very clean, which is important for a good night's rest.

Clothes Storage

As we've mentioned previously, we have a lot of clothes; we need both dress clothes and casual. So for our clothes storage, we decided to have it all in the second loft. This, for us, was the best option for our space. With the loft being 7 feet deep, we decided to have a clothes hanging rod as deep as the loft is. If this plan of using our second loft didn't work as planned to hang clothes—for instance, if climbing up and down the loft ladder felt as though it was getting old and we just didn't like it as much as we thought we would—then we had planned on creating a space in the bathroom where the washer/dryer combo is and using it as an enclosed wardrobe. Thankfully, Plan A has worked out great for us, and climbing the short distance up to our closet loft hasn't been an issue; we generally only

go up once a day, as we have decided to keep our pajamas in the floor storage in the master loft. Each night we are able to put our dirty clothes in the bathroom hamper and throw those that are not dirty in the second closet loft. We then hang and fold them the next day when we go up into the loft. Or, sometimes, we're feeling less lazy and go up a second time into the closet loft to actually hang our clothes and fold them; it really isn't as bad going in and out of the second loft as we thought it would be. It's only four steps on the ladder and takes a second to get up there. We were used to small closets in our previous home, which were actually close to the same amount of space as we currently have in the 7-feet deep space; we really didn't have to sacrifice our hanging clothes space. We do rotate our clothes depending on the seasons. In the summer, out go the big fluffy coats and scarfs, and in the winter, the summer dresses and short-sleeved shirts get put away. We vacuum pack these clothes that we rotate and store them in one of our small, outdoor plastic containers. In the beginning, we thought we would pare down our clothes to just a few outfits per season and not have to rotate our clothes, but who are we kidding. We love clothes and our accessories, and we knew we couldn't just get rid of them—we would find a way to squeeze it all in. So when in a small space, those clothes storage bags are a lifesaver. For our folded clothes, we moved them into the second loft with the hanging clothes. We got four sets of two drawers, equaling eight drawers. These hold as much or more than the floor cubby storage did. It was more functional for us to have all of our clothes, both folded and hanging, in one loft. We're also able to utilize the space on top of the sets of drawers for additional hat, purse, or shoe storage. There's also the vanity in between these two clothes areas, and underneath the makeup vanity which stores several other girly things, such as jewelry and craft supplies. At the end of the set of drawers there's also a small space that holds extra craft supplies and other random goods.

Under Stair Storage

Most of us have seen the ever popular cubby stairs storage. These are a great option for those who must have a certain amount of storage. Why did we choose not to do cubby stairs storage? While they are very functional, we didn't want to have that main area of our house feel narrow and closed in. We still wanted a staircase that is a normal width of 24 inches; however, to have that full amount of space enclosed would make the house feel quite a bit more closed in. Since we've seen several houses in person after building ours that did have the stair cubby storage, it made us that much happier that we chose not to do it. While we have nothing against them and they are great for a good amount of storage, for our space it would have changed the feel tremendously. When we were looking for alternate stair options, we found someone on YouTube in New Zealand who had metal stairs, and we loved how there was a visual pass through the stairs. Since we have experience in metal fabrication, we knew we wanted to incorporate some industrial aspect into our design. Adding the wood steps on top of the metal warms up the space and our feet as we walk up and down them. As for below the stairs, we still wanted some storage. Since the wheel well is below the stairs, we worked to have shelving and storage that was only as deep as the wheel well, which is

about 10 inches. By having the storage only 10 inches deep and not the full 24 inches of the stairs, it allows a visual pass through the metal stairs but also allows us to have plenty of useful storage, something we wouldn't have if we had chosen closed-in cubby stairs. In this space, we've gone through several options of storage; we've had several types of bins and baskets. This space also changes on a fairly regular basis depending on our needs at the time, including gear for the winter, such as coats, scarfs, and boots, which take up a good amount of space. We tend to store our camera gear, some shoes, purses, and other miscellaneous items under the stairs. We have also added a long ottoman that has storage inside to hold some gear; this ottoman fits nicely under the stairs and allows us to prop our feet up when watching TV or relaxing by the fire. We also rotate and shift items between the utility closet and underneath the stairs. Both will store office gear adequately, and we arrange them to fit our seasonal needs. We basically arrange things in a way that makes sense at the time, and when it no longer works, we change it!

Exterior Storage

Unless you are master of downsizing, chances are you will still have some necessary items that will need to be stored outside the tiny house or offsite. These can be anything from garden tools, bicycles, camping gear... the list can go on from there. When we started our downsizing process, we knew we would realistically need outdoor storage for some of our things. In our last house, we had a large number of tools and equipment that would still make their way to the tiny house. Yes, we were committed to drastically downsizing our living space, but we still had many things that needed to come along with us. We applaud all who have been able to downsize their belongings into a tiny house, but for this life change, we needed to be practical.

To aid with storage directly outside of our tiny house, we designed some storage closets that could be built under our deck seating. This would serve to store lesser-used items, like garden tools, axes, and firewood. With every storage solution, there is always a trade-off; the deck storage did provide a good amount of space to store things, but the ease of access was hard and we ended up not using it all that often. It also closed off the deck from our view outside; we preferred to look out onto our yard versus looking back at our house, so we decided to remove the storage benches and add steps walking out into our yard for a more inviting entrance. On the back side of the tiny house, we added some smaller plastic storage totes that could hold other small items we kept outside, like dog gear, tools for our water system, and other items we couldn't fit in the under-deck storage.

But what about the big stuff? I mean, we had A LOT of stuff. For the first year, we thought we would use all the things we had (or at least that is what we thought). We had a storage unit for the first year of living tiny. We finally put overcame our procrastination, eliminated that stuff and got down to only the things we needed. What we didn't use in the past year either got sold or donated and the rest of the things we used on a regular basis were brought back with us to the tiny house. Downsizing is a process, and for some people it can take years to get it down to what makes the most sense. We were the same way; we would try something and see if it worked, and if it didn't we would improve and change as needed. We knew early on we would need a workshop or garage to store all the personal items we couldn't store inside our tiny house, but as to the size, we didn't quite know yet (remember, downsizing is a process). In the beginning, we purchased a heavy-duty carport and installed it over a level gravel pad with shelving and a workbench. This has ended up working until this day. Inside the carport we have plenty of storage for all of our welding and car mechanic tools. Loads and loads of camping gear and other seasonal items, like fans, small heaters, and clothes, plus leftover building materials that we still use for projects, are stored here. Downsizing down to this level was a huge undertaking and a lot of work, and we are definitely not done. We will always refine and always change to adapt to our needs better.

CHAPTER 7

Pets In A Tiny House

A LOT OF PEOPLE HAVE PETS and love their beloved furballs, us included! So when we decided to downsize and go tiny, we thought it would be a challenge to figure out how we were all going to work in a much smaller space. It seemed to be more of a mental challenge than a physical one. We were already downsizing with all of our stuff from 1,300 square feet to 374 square feet! Was it practical to think that we could work two small dogs into the space along with all of our junk? Was it going to drive us completely insane to have these two little furballs by our feet all the time? Where would they sleep? Where would we keep their dog food, toys, bowls, etc.? We had a lot of questions rolling around in our minds. Were we crazy to think we could have pets with us in our small space. Not having them wasn't even an option for us; we knew we would find a way to make it work. The question was always about comfort. Not just our comfort, but as any pet parent knows, their comfort. We were surprised to find out just how well and easily we adapted to having the pets in our small space.

One Of Our Bigger Obstacles

Everyone is different with their pets and habits. Each will also have different challenges when downsizing. One of our biggest challenges was figuring out what to do with our dogs when we were gone from the house. Letting them have free rein and sleep in our bed wasn't an option. They were crate trained and are used to sleeping in a crate at night, as well as when we leave for errands. Another challenge in a small space was the muddy paws after a nice rain. There aren't many options for keeping them sectioned off without having a large bulky gate that can't be hidden or a big space hog of a dog crate. This was a challenge when in our 1,300-square foot home and became an even larger challenge when we moved into our 374-square foot tiny home!

So what did we do to crate our dogs while we went out for errands or to keep them from muddying the house? Initially, we used a bulky baby gate that was unattractive and took up precious space. Since this clearly wasn't going to work long-term, we had to find something else that would be slim, sleek, and tiny house friendly. We were then excited to stumble on a product called Retract-A-Gate. For starters, it's attractive when in use and practically invisible when not in use. It is 34 inches tall and can fit an opening up to 72 inches wide. The height fits right under a standard countertop. It has a tough and washable see-through mesh barrier, which helps the dogs not feel so closed off from us. We use ours to section the pups off in the kitchen area. It comes in several colors, including black, white, and beige. We have the black one. The retractable gate is proven durable for dogs (or kids), and automatically and quietly rewinds to a small roll when not in use. It can be removed and reinstalled instantly to other locations with an additional universal mounting bracket kit. It has a child and pet safety lock that opens or closes with a childproof feature. In addition, it works great outdoors on decks, porches, boats, motor homes, and, of course, tiny houses. Having this gate has been our lasting solution to what was our single biggest challenge. With the biggest concern tackled and out of the way, what about all the other little challenges of having pets in a small space?

Adapting To Pets In A Small Space

Since the space is small and the dogs are sectioned off with their pet gate in the kitchen while sleeping at night and while we're gone, how do they do in the space when we're home? During the day when we're home, it's like musical chairs for us. Since our two dogs are small and they share a bed, it makes things a little easier. We tend to move the bed around the tiny house as we need to; since we do cook and need the kitchen, the dogs need to be out of that space for the majority of the day. So we do just that, and move them usually in front of the wood burning stove across from the couch in the "living room" area when the stove isn't burning. When we want to watch TV and get extra comfy, we move our storage ottoman over to put our feet up, moving the dog bed over to where the ottoman was. Wherever their bed goes, they go.

When we need to let the dogs expend energy, they play on the property while on extra-long leashes. In addition, we have a drone that they LOVE to chase. We also take them to dog parks and on walks.

Has Living In A Small Space Made The Pets Sedentary Or Lazy?

One thing we were concerned about with a smaller space was whether it would make our already sometimes lazy pets even lazier than they tend to be. It was a legitimate concern since they would no longer have the extra space to run around in the house and wrestle from room to room. What we have found, however, is that it doesn't matter what size the space is—their habits will still be the same no matter where we go. We have seen this as we've traveled across the US and have been in many different-sized spaces along the way, including lots of camping with the dogs sleeping in the tent with us. They still wrestle anywhere they can. They move all around the bottom floor of the tiny house, roughhousing and sleeping wherever they feel most comfortable at the moment, bathroom included. They still stick close by our feet, which was the case in our bigger house also. When it's really rainy and they can't play outside as much as we would like them to, we improvise and throw their toys across the length of the tiny house. Pets are very adaptable and take the same amount of care regardless of the size space you live in. The obstacle is usually a mental one for humans, thinking our pets need a certain space or situation to be comfortable, when in reality, they just want to be near us wherever they live.

Pets And Stairs

Since we have stairs that lead up to our main sleeping loft, we often get asked if the dogs have any problems getting up the stairs and if they have problems with getting down the stairs. Unfortunately for us... no, no they don't at all. We personally don't like having our dogs in our sleeping loft and don't want them sleeping in our bed. We make exceptions when they've just gotten a bath and if we've been out of the house longer than planned while they're crated. In that instance, we will allow our furballs to sleep in the loft at night so we don't have to deal with one of them who has a bit of separation anxiety, barking all night and depriving us of any sleep. Our dogs aren't perfect and neither are we at training, so sometimes barking at night can be an issue when we've been gone all day. One day we'll get it figured out; until then, that's the arrangement we have in place from time to time.

We have absolutely nothing against anyone who likes having their pets snuggle in bed with them; our pets, however, become bed hogs, and that is annoying. So, we prefer them to be crated while we sleep and are gone. When we first moved into the tiny house, the dogs were not allowed to use the stairs and didn't even attempt going up. This was a blissful several first months for us, as we wanted the loft off limits anyway. Our dogs are a small 20 pounds each, so we imagine that larger dogs or even cats would have no problem figuring out how to climb up and down those stairs instantly. Once our dogs figured out going up and down was a breeze, it was a challenge to keep them from trying to climb them every second we weren't looking. More dog training to be done, yay. After some effort we got them mostly trained to not go up there when we're home and not looking. Since our master loft is open without any railing at the edge, we have also often wondered if they might fall off the edge. The answer is no. Pets are much smarter than we give them credit for, and just as they can detect when something is hot and shy away from it, they also can detect when a ledge is too high to jump off of. Our dogs don't even lie too close to that edge; they are smart enough to know it's too high. From the edge of our bed to the edge of the loft there are 5 feet, giving them plenty of space to stretch out without getting close to the edge. If you plan on having your pets in your loft with you and are afraid that they might fall off the edge, then you can certainly add a railing or half/full wall to ensure their safety. It hasn't been an issue for us, but they also are only allowed up there when we are, so we can keep an eye out for them just in case. If you really don't want your pets in your loft, then you can always go the ladder route. That will ensure your pets can't get up there, unless you have amazingly trained pets that are skilled enough to climb a ladder; in that case, we would like to hire you to train our pets.

Washing A Dog In A Tiny House

We've always liked the option of washing our dogs at home in-between groomings. It saves money and time. Maybe you have pets who don't need to be groomed at all; we envy you if that's the case. For us poor souls who picked pets that are forever growing hair and need some regular TLC, it's a nice option to be able to wash your pet at home rather than having to take them elsewhere. But can it be done in a tiny house? This will depend on the size of your pet and the type of shower or tub you decide to go with in your tiny house. Since we decided to go with a shower, it proved to be a bit of a challenge at first. In our previous house, we had a bathtub, which made it easier to bathe the dogs. When designing the tiny house, however, we decided to have a shower with a glass enclosure for optimal space in the bathroom. We chose a good-sized corner shower that is 39 inches, which gives us plenty of room to wash up while in it. However, we didn't even think about the dogs when we were designing the bathroom. So we came up with a couple of options to wash them depending on time and season. When it's nice and warm outside, we have the option to just bathe them right outside; even just on the deck works well for us since we can leash them while we bathe them. The option apart from grooming is taking them to a pet store; some have self-dog washes that tend to run about $10 to $15 for a given amount of time. We're able to wash and dry both of our dogs in that time slot. The last option, if it's not so nice out and when we simply don't have time to get to the pet store to wash them, is washing them in our shower. Sounds tricky, right? Well, it was at first, then we figured out a way that works for us. Just a heads up, this way might not work for everyone—it's all dependent on your pets and their size and demeanor. What's proved to work really well for us is for each of us to take a dog into the shower with us and close the glass door. Yep—we have to hop in and just close the glass door, otherwise they try to walk out with the door open. Sounds weird, we know, but it's actually been quite easy and fast. Since we have a handheld shower handle, it makes it much easier to wash the dogs thoroughly and quickly with the spray nozzle. We wash the dogs and turn the shower head off and towel dry them, then let them hang out in the bathroom and shake off while we shower ourselves after. We

put a couple of dog towels down so they have something to rub on while we shower. After they've air dried a bit, out comes the blow dryer. Since the bathroom is small, cleanup is a breeze and takes very little time to wipe down. These are a few ways that have worked for us personally with bathing dogs in the tiny house.

When A Tiny House With Pets Does Feel Small...

There have only been a handful of times when our place has felt very small, and those few times have been related to pets. Now, this is a very rare situation, but we figured we might as well share the experience anyway. Since we live in a country setting, our neighbors consist mostly of wildlife, and with that, some of these wildlife neighbors happen to be skunks. Now, both of our dogs really get along with cats and other dogs quite well, and we genuinely feel that they have mistaken those little stinky mammals on several occasions for friendly kitties in the same way Pepé Le Pew mistakes Penelope Pussycat for a skunk like himself. On two separate occasions while letting the dogs out at night, they have both (a different dog each time) discovered a skunk, and knowing the personalities of these dogs really well, we know they likely tried to play around with the little skunkies and their advances were not welcomed. The worst of these instances was on a stormy night, and our smaller cockapoo June could not be found and, when we located her, we smelled the problem immediately. We took appropriate action and bathed her the recommended way according to the SPCA which helped a ton, but the smell lingered for quite some time even after many baths. This stinky episode really made our little home feel way too small. After all, it was winter, and the dogs needed to be inside—and when they were inside, you just couldn't escape the smell! Now, we wish we could offer some advice to help with this, but it is what it is sometimes. Situations come up that you don't expect and you just adapt to make do with what you have. No matter the square footage, there will be situations that will make your home feel small or cramped. We had cabin fever in our old house during the winter months, and that was 1,300 square feet; if only we knew then that we would be comfortable a few years down the line in only 374 square feet. Granted, if the dogs ever get skunked again, we may just have to ship them off to a doggy spa until they are clean.

Other Types Of Pets

So, what if you have a cat or another type of pet that you want to have in a tiny house? Can it be done? Since we only have two dogs in our tiny house, we can mainly only speak from the experience we have with them. However, when we were going tiny initially, we had both an outdoor cat and indoor/outdoor cat. We still have our outdoor cat and she does great. She is very quick and loves the outdoors. We tried making her an indoor cat at one point in our previous home, but that did not go well, at all. We also had an indoor/outdoor cat that we were planning on incorporating into the tiny house and design. Because she was a very domesticated cat that was used to the suburbs and not very fast at all, and we were moving to an area where there was more wildlife, we knew trying to keep her only indoors would be a big challenge as we had already tried and failed. So, we ended up giving her to family. However, it did have us planning and thinking in the beginning how we could incorporate an indoor cat. We've seen many people with tiny houses have cats successfully in their small spaces. Since we didn't end up having to plan around having a cat, we'll just be speaking in hypotheticals. Now living in a tiny house and interacting in the space, we can't help but think how we would have had an indoor cat work. One of the first things we thought about was where a cat box would go so that it wouldn't be messy and smelly. Originally, we wanted an enclosure to be built out on the tongue off the bathroom for a cat box with a flap that the cat would have to go through to keep the odor and mess separate. We would still choose to do a cat box off of the bathroom if we ever decided to get an indoor cat. We've seen many with cubby storage stairs incorporate a litter box into one of the cubbies that have had good success. Since a tiny house with lofts is tall and kind of like a tree house anyway, those with cats seem to not have much of a problem with a need for a cat tree since they have stairs to climb and sometimes upper storage areas to hide in. The only time we have had to bring our cat in is on rare occasions in winter when temperatures dip down too low. In that case, we bring her up to the second clothes loft where she can snuggle up and feel hidden. In those few cases, we still let her outside to use the bathroom since that is what she's used to.

There are many ways to incorporate pets into your small space, and if you already have pets, you'll know what they already like and will be able to get crafty in your design to make it work for them and, more importantly, work for you. We've been pleasantly surprised as to how well the pets work in the space, and it doesn't feel at all cramped with them. Pets are very adaptable, and you too will be surprised at how easy a transition it will be. Just figuring out a few key things that work for you and your living situation will be helpful in a small space and will reduce frustrations. There's always going to be a little trial and error getting into a routine in any new living situation, regardless of the size.

CHAPTER 8

Relationships In Tight Quarters

MAYBE NOW YOU'RE TO THE POINT where you've decided that you can in fact see yourself downsizing and living in a tiny house or a much smaller space than you are currently in. However, you may have a spouse or even children to consider as well. So, can it be done? Can you successfully have a good marriage or relationship in such a small space? Or will being in that small space be the straw that breaks the camel's back and your relationship? This is one of the MOST frequently asked questions we get on a daily basis, from complete strangers to even family and friends. "How do you guys do it??!!" Well, we will tell you what's worked for us, what needs working on, and whether we recommend it.

Full disclaimer: We are in no way relationship experts and are not here to write a self-help or relationships chapter. We are purely here to convey what's worked and hasn't worked for us and why, in hopes it'll be a guide to help you decide whether tiny living may or may not be for you.

Having A Solid Foundation, Beneficial For More Than Just A House

We discussed in the previous chapters how important it is to have a solid foundation for our homes, whether it be on a trailer for a tiny house on wheels or on a solid personal foundation. It is the first and most important step. Without having a solid foundation, the rest of the build won't matter or last long-term. The same goes for our relationships, whether it is with our spouse, family members, or friends. When we were in our planning phase of going tiny, of course one of our main thoughts and concerns was, "Are we going to be able to be around each other in such a small space all the time without wanting to snap at each other on a regular basis?!" Ultimately when you're a couple deciding to downsize, one of the main thoughts will be whether it'll be practical or reasonable to put yourselves in that small space together, and whether you're the types who can handle it. There is a whole lot of self-evaluation that happens and needs to happen when deciding to downsize this drastically. Sometimes it can be a less than fun experience to self-evaluate and realize that maybe we aren't the most cool, calm, and collected perfect specimens that we thought we were, and that's ok. One of the most important steps in this process is to be humble and set our pride aside to realize that we might have some small personal changes to make. Being humble in this somewhat bizarre transition will be key to making it successful.

When we decided we were going to make our tiny house living dreams happen it was beyond exciting and equally scary, because we all know what our limits are as individuals and we can easily envision ourselves in a space. But the real challenge comes when we try to envision our spouse and/or other family members interacting in a space with us. We knew there were going to be adjustments and challenges when it came to downsizing and living with each other in a small space. But what made us know that we could successfully live together in a small space situation was that we had a solid foundation in our marriage. We work hard to regularly apply the practical advice found in the Bible to love and respect one another. Whether you're one who believes in the Bible or not, you can still appreciate the practical advice of 1 Corinthians 13:4-5, 7 that says, "Love is patient and kind. Love is not jealous. It does not brag, does not get puffed up, does not behave indecently, does not look for its own interests, does not become provoked. It does not keep account of the injury. It bears all things, believes all things, hopes all things, and endures all things. Love never fails." Working on those qualities regularly in our marriage helps build a stronger and stronger foundation. While we don't always apply them perfectly and have better days than others, keeping these qualities in mind and making a conscious effort to apply them has really helped us to be considerate of one another. Being considerate of the other person goes a long way when in a tiny house or any small space that you'll be sharing with someone.

How Being In A Small Space Has Actually Helped Our Communication

We all know and hear often that communication is key for a functional relationship, which is so very true. This will be even truer in a small space. We often get asked if being in this small of a space makes us want to strangle one another. Sure, we have our moments, we are human after all. But more than often, what we have found is that being in a small space has made us have to talk things out more. There's no door to slam when irritated, there's not really an "other side of the house" to go to for isolation. It's all right in front you. When the other person is upset you know and can feel it. In our old house, when we would get irritated or get into it, we could easily go into separate rooms and close the door and ignore each other for hours. While, depending on the conflict and the severity of it, we recognize that sometimes we need to take some time to cool down and get our heads together in order to talk it out without yelling, we've also found that being in the smaller space and knowing we can't go isolate ourselves in separate rooms for hours like we used to has actually helped each of us to get over things much faster. We try to work hard to just let it go. Usually the issue we're arguing about isn't that big to begin with or worth the dramatic fight that could easily escalate, which would mean a very tense and awkward tiny house situation. The more you're in a small space together, the more you learn that some things really just aren't worth nitpicking over and fighting about. You both realize quickly what irritating quirks you have as an individual, and so can see even more how they could be irritating to someone else. So we have actually have been able to work on our flaws more because we see things about ourselves that we never realized when in a larger space.

What About When You Need A Little Alone Time?

We all need our space from time to time, and depending on our personality or current stresses, may need more alone time. So, what do we do for our alone time? There are several options, and they really don't differ too much from any other living situation, except for a couple of exceptions. In our tiny house, we do have two lofts up above the main floor. Our sleeping loft, which is 12 feet deep, is surprisingly pretty private since it is so deep. When up there, we're not able to see the other person down below; of course you can still hear each other since we don't have a dividing wall, but even not seeing the other person makes it feel as though you're there alone. If you or your spouse is really loud and you need actual quiet time and not just alone time, then you might want to consider closing the upper loft off for extra quiet and privacy. That's not something that bothers us personally, so just being in separate spaces of the tiny house has worked out great for us. We also have the second loft that we essentially use as a closet, but sometimes one of us will go up there with a computer and do work just to mix up the spaces. From that vantage point, we can't see the other person if they are sitting on the couch. The second loft isn't quite as private, but it's nice just to mix up spaces and work stations sometimes. Then there's also the option of going outside. We have areas outside to just sit and relax, and this is definitely a great option to get out of your space and get some fresh air and vitamin D if the sun is out, but also to have some quiet time. Then there's also the option of getting away from the tiny house altogether, doing your own errands or spending time out and away doing something you enjoy. It's pretty much the same type of thing as when you live in any space. You still have your routine and that doesn't change a whole lot being in a smaller space; you just have less junk in your house to deal with.

When You're A Couple Who Works Together

There is a category of couples who work together, or where one works from home and the other is a stay at home spouse or parent. How does tiny house living affect these couples? Well, we are one of those couples who work together and are living in a tiny house. We'll go a little more in-depth here, as we have first-hand experience with it. We've talked to many who want to downsize, and they also have ideas and goals to work from home in order to simplify and reduce the stresses of being in an office. So how is working together in tight quarters?

   First, a quick little story. When we got married, we started working together; however, due to the nature of the business at that time, we were rarely actually together working. Once we downsized the business, we did end up actually working closely day in and day out. We had that business for the next couple of years, working closely together, and this was probably the toughest time due to the transition and being around one another for most of the day. Dealing with work stresses together and making decisions together was also tough at times. We did, however, have some time to get into a good flow and work out kinks that happen when you are so close to someone all the time. We feel it's important to mention this period and transition time because it won't be easy at first if you work together or are planning to start your own small business as a couple. We had this time to adapt to working together before we decided to go tiny. In fact, once we got past the initial frustrations of being a couple who worked together and got into a routine, we realized that we could do it. This is when we became even more interested in downsizing. We realized that we already had the stress of being small business owners and that we didn't want to come home and have a larger house to take care of. As we got out of our previous line of work and started our Tiny House Trailer business and our website www.TinyHouseBasics.com, we ended up still working closely together, but it involved a lot less driving around time which was less stress. We were still working closely together, just mainly on computers now. We are still around each other most of the time. So, how has working in a small space been? There are pros and cons to every situation. We feel the pros and cons are pretty much the same as if we were in our previous 1,300 square foot house. The pros are that we have the option to stay in all day if we need to in order to get things done and that we don't have to deal with the general public and with people bugging us. Also being in our smaller space, we have less to worry about and maintain; we're also able to mix up where we work even at home in a small space. Depending on how we feel, we can lay in bed and do computer work or sit at our large 8-foot accordion/bi-fold window, which is where we are most times. One of us sometimes even sits up in the second closet loft just to mix it up. Of course there's the comfy couch to sit on, also. When the weather is nice, we take it outside to get some fresh air. Sometimes one of us will stay in and one of us will go outside just out of personal preference at the time. Since we do work in the small space together, we do find that having the two lofts has been very helpful in that it does create separate spaces even if they are open. We mentioned earlier that when one is in the sleeping loft we can't see each other when the other is downstairs. It really does feel like a separate space, which has been helpful.

The downsides of working at home in any sized space we feel can be the same. While it's great to have the option of being home all day, it can get old being in one location all day long. When we start to feel antsy, we pack up our computers and head to coffee shops or parks to change our scenery. We had to do this even in our larger house. Any space starts to feel confining when there too long. Many go into offices for work, and even if they have a large office, it too starts to feel small when they're there so many hours a day. So as long as you keep a realistic view about varying your work location, it'll be just fine working from home. As a couple working together, we can tell when we've been cooped up for too long; we start getting irritated and snippy with one another much faster. That's when we have to recognize that we need to get out of our small space to be productive. The key is being balanced with most things. This is a constant effort for us.

Fights In A Tiny House:
Does A Small Space Mean More Frequent Fights?

Now to the nitty-gritty, not-so-fun stuff: fights, arguments, and disagreements. Whatever you want to call them, they happen. We're all imperfect; therefore, we will get on each other's nerves at some point. This is true regardless of the square footage of your home. This is a big concern for those truly considering downsizing. We were the same; we had never lived in this small of a space together before and weren't sure how we would react. You can imagine and try to envision it all you want. Until you live in it, you'll never know or be able to predict how you'll interact in the space. So, how has it affected us and has it made us fight more? Surprisingly, no; as we mentioned before, the smaller space has actually taught us to communicate more. You absolutely have to, and there is no way of getting around it. You MUST take your stubborn pants off and learn to relax and let things go. Otherwise, be prepared for walking on eggshells in a small space. Despite the fact that it has helped us communicate better, we do still have our moments. This will of course depend on what life events are going on and what other stressors you currently have to deal with.

Money: One of the main things couples fight about is money. Money and how to spend it and the lack of it is usually a root of many frustrations. It's a domino effect; we need money to survive, yet we have to kill ourselves to work for it. Then, once we get it, we don't even get to spend it on something fun or anything we want, but rather it goes to bills. Naturally, when we're working hard all day—and usually not doing something we enjoy—we're sleep deprived, and come home to another person who is just as stressed or grumpy for the very same reasons. Then at the end of the week, when it seems we get a break and we get to regroup and do something we enjoy...oh wait, we've just spent our hard-earned money on bills, usually with the largest portion going to the home we live in. Now we have a little left over, but we both have different ideas of how we want to spend it. Here comes the tension.

This all too familiar situation can add frustrations, and often leaves us asking ourselves why we work so hard for a place that we are never in and never get to enjoy. Of course, we need a place to live, and this expense of owning or renting isn't optional. It truly becomes a double-edged sword, and often is the source of many disagreements. If you've found yourself in this same mental cycle, then take comfort in knowing that downsizing and simplifying will most definitely help those tensions and disagreements lessen tremendously. Having a lower living cost and getting to enjoy the fruits of your labor, or even having the ability to save money, will help lessen those disagreements and their frequency.

Tension When Building

Building projects are stressful even when small. You both might have ideas regarding the final outcome, and sometimes getting on the same page is hard. We have always felt that we have similar tastes and that made some things easier; however, men and women have different needs and priorities in a living situation. This is where some tension can arise. Add the financial restrictions and then a deadline and you've got yourself a prime situation to have a heated discussion. As long as you know that this can be a tense time and you mentally prepare for it, then being ok with the fact that you might have some disagreements won't be so bad. Prepare for the worst and hope for the best. This planning and building phase and the tensions and stresses that can come with it will pass, and the end product and lifestyle will absolutely be worth those disagreements.

Getting Into A New Routine In A Small Space

There is going to be a bit of a learning curve when in a tiny house just as there would be when moving to any new space. So if any disagreements are going to happen, they likely will occur during this transition time. Since the space was so different from any other space we had lived in before, adapting to less storage space and realizing that a lot of stuff still needed to be eliminated caused some tension in the beginning. It can get easy to point the finger at the other and think they have too much stuff, when in reality you both do. The process of downsizing can be stressful since we emotionally get attached to items. It can be easy to take out our frustrations on our spouse and convince ourselves that the other one is to blame because they have too much stuff. This is when we all have to dig deep and remember we need LOTS AND LOTS of compromise and being humble and reasonable with each other without being prideful and stubborn and always digging in our heels; this makes any disagreements smooth over much faster. Our suggestion: get rid of as much as possible

before moving into your tiny house. Once you get in it, you'll realize just how many extra items aren't needed or even used and arguments out of frustration from not downsizing enough beforehand can be avoided alltogether. We learned the hard way, and now we can't even remember what items we used to argue about not wanting to get rid of. Remember these moments will be temporary, and just expect it to happen sometime in this transition. Before you know it, you'll be adapted and have less stress from less items, and your new routine will be second nature.

Our Surprising Reality

Living in a smaller space hasn't caused more arguments despite what we thought. We'll be honest: we didn't know how we were going to react in such a small space when we decided to go ahead with it. We like to think we're cool as cucumbers and can take on anything, but in reality, if you stick any of us in an unfamiliar situation, that's when some ugly sides can come out. Once you get your routine down, it'll be just like any living situation. You're still going to get on each other's nerves sometimes, you're still going to have your moments when you want to be left alone, and you're still going to want things done your way sometimes, even if you know it's not reasonable. We are who we are, and being in a small space doesn't change that. What does change or help is that you are forced to do a regular self-evaluation in a small space, because everything is right in front facing you. Your spouse, your stuff that you own, your mess, your quirks, everything. You and your spouse ultimately know what you can handle and how you interact now with each other won't change too much. It may get better if your main stresses are financial and wanting more time for things you enjoy. If you're feeling like you must go tiny out of necessity but both or one of you isn't at all excited about it, then be prepared for some trials and tribulations. We were both very excited to do this; it meant more than just a lessened financial burden, it meant we got to live a more simple life and that would be more meaningful to us. Also a big bonus...less cleaning! We were on the same page of being sick of striving to maintain material items; therefore, even though we knew it would be an adjustment, it would be worth it in the long run. We can say after being in the tiny house for many years now that it has in fact helped our love and marriage grow, and it has helped us with our communication. Being realistic in your expectations and knowing that you're still going to have trials from life at times will help in making your simplifying process go smoothly. If you're both excited about tiny living and you get along for the most part, but one of your bigger hesitations is the fear of it straining your relationship, we say go for it and give it a try. You'll be surprised about the positive effect it'll have and how much you can grow together because of it.

Our priority was making memories over money, and going tiny and simplifying has been one of the best decisions we have made for our well-being and our relationship. We don't regret it one bit.

CHAPTER 9

The Rewards, Benefits, And Challenges Of Downsizing

WHEN MAKING ANY BIG LIFE DECISION, it is best to always calculate the cost, not only in a monetary aspect, but how it will affect your life as a whole. When downsizing your life, some of the more popular rewards and benefits can be easily seen, but what are the challenges? There are obvious challenges, both mentally and physically. We are all individuals and we will all react to things differently, but for this part of our story, we are going to share the rewards, benefits, and the challenges we faced when going tiny.

Rewards

One of the biggest rewards was the money that was staying in our pocket and not going to rent or a mortgage. It can be easy to quickly grasp the monetary advantages of living in a smaller space; a smaller square footage usually equals less in rent or mortgage—that is unless we are talking about San Francisco or Manhattan, where it seems to be expensive no matter the square footage! There are some amazing small spaces in cities across the country where the cost benefits enable people

to live in the heart of a city that normally would have been expensive. No way were we going to be able to continue to live in the Bay Area if we did not drastically change how we were living. As the years went by, housing just got more and more expensive, but the wages seemed to always stay the same. Real estate trends continue to show they will rise through the decades ahead. When we look at the median rental prices in our old neighborhood, we reaffirm that we made the right decision at the right time. Money and the pursuit of it can easily cause a massive amount of stress in your life; it did for us. We were not pursuing money for the fun of it; the pursuit was just so we could keep our heads above water and be able to pay our bills and have the cash flow to do the things we loved. Money, after all, is one of the most common things couples can fight about. The purpose of living is not to accumulate stuff no matter what our modern day society would like us to believe. This is not to say when we downsized to our tiny house our worries were over; like we mentioned in previous chapters, there was a recovery period from the expense of our custom tiny house build. We still have the troubles and worries that many people face today; it is just the high cost of living is absolutely not one of them. It has been a big relief to alleviate at least one of life's biggest worries, but it's still no gravy train with biscuit wheels.

Benefits

The benefits of tiny living are seemingly endless; by choosing to live tiny, we chose to live deliberately. We chose our line of work to fit our new lifestyle. We choose when we work, when we vacation, and when we focus on our other activities that bring us joy. By living in a small footprint, it allows us to spend less, use less, and stress less. Many people are drawn to tiny houses because it creates that freedom of being able to travel anywhere with their home; and yes, it is very true you can do that—you can travel anywhere your heart desires if that is your plan. For us, we never intended to travel with our tiny house; we meant to travel because of it. In our first few years of marriage living in our "gigantic" 1,300-square foot house, we traveled here and there, maybe a few times a year. On our first anniversary, we traveled a few hours north to Fort Bragg and Mendocino, but that trip was only limited to four days due to our work commitments. On our second anniversary, we traveled south to Santa Barbara, and once again that trip was cut short due to work. This trip was also a breaking point, where we decided to reevaluate the work we were doing and how it was impacting the very little free time we had. This trip was when we started the process of downsizing our work, and we let a few clients go due to their unreasonable requests and demands for our time. On our third anniversary, we traveled the farthest we have ever gone since being married, up to Washington state and our tiny house story began. This was a turning point for us. We desired to live a more modest life, and have a life that was kept in moderation. We were not balanced up to that point and it was painfully obvious; the stress of making a living in this modern age was wearing us down. That next year was when we built our tiny house. That first year of tiny house living we traveled a lot (not with the tiny house). We had a low cost of living and free time like we never had before; our life was becoming more about living and not just working. That first year we traveled across many states, but we were also very happy to come back home to our tiny house. Our second full year living tiny allowed us even more freedom. For our five year anniversary, we decided on a whim to do a road trip. We couldn't narrow down where we wanted to go, so we decided to go to every city on our list in the US. With less than a month of planning, we packed up our pick-up, paid our rent for the months we would be gone, loaded up the poodles and set off. We were on the road for just over six weeks, and we traveled through thirty-three states on our cross-country adventure, from California to New Orleans, New York City to Maine, Chicago to Kentucky, Nashville to Yellowstone. We had one amazing adventure of a lifetime, and it won't be our last. One of the important things we learned about ourselves on our road trip is that while we love our tiny house, we wouldn't want to travel with it. As much as we loved the adventure of being on the road, we loved having a home base to go back to. A sense of routine is nice and you don't have that on the road, but we do always

have that option to pack up and hit the road for a month. Our tiny house has afforded us this freedom and living deliberately has allowed us to choose a line of work (which happens to be building tiny houses and trailers) that doesn't dictate where we are or how we spend our time.

With the freedom a tiny house creates, you never have to worry about any future moves. One of the struggles with buying a house (besides the cost) is the permanence in settling down. With a tiny house, you have your home but you can change the view you see out the window anytime you please. Even if you set up your house as a "base camp" and plan to travel because of it and not with it, you can still move your home base every couple of years or as frequently as you would like. We love where we have our tiny house parked and couldn't imagine ever changing our view, but that option is always there. Unless you buy the land for your tiny house you have no ties to the land itself, just the house. If you decide to make a job change or a move to another city, you can just hitch up the house and find a new home; granted, you will still need to find a new place to park.

Another benefit when building or living in a tiny house is you can be environmentally-friendly. When searching for a traditional home to

rent or buy, you have no input on what materials were used to build the house since it's already built. Even when building your own full-size home, the cost of using greener products can multiply the budget exponentially. With a tiny home, the footprint is small, so you can reuse materials, windows and finishes to keep the cost down, but also be more environmentally-friendly. We do, however, always recommend new lumber for framing, sheathing, and structural components. Old structural wood is usually compromised by warping, insect damage, or other factors, so while they're not suitable to carry loads, they can be installed in a way that makes them look as though they're doing the work. But even with new products there are green alternatives that are sustainably harvested and grown. There are also advances in the types of plywood and OSB available that do not use formaldehyde in their glues, which limits the hazardous chemicals in your small home. Reclaimed woods for siding and flooring are becoming more abundant and readily available. In our tiny house, we originally used a laminate-type flooring which has not held up well; we will be removing it and replacing it with one-hundred-year-old reclaimed barn oak flooring. Along with renewable and environmentally-friendly materials, you can also set up your tiny house to be more energy

efficient by getting its power supply from a solar panel system, or even small wind generators. If you live in a rainy climate, you can even build the roof to be a rain catch system, filtering the water and reusing it. For the plumbing, you can install a composting toilet to minimize the waste water you use and allow you to park your tiny house anywhere and not be limited by the utilities present.

Decluttering Your Life

You have to, you have no choice. You can only fit so much in 400 or so square feet. This a major benefit but it can come with some resistance; we fought it all the way. We thought we needed everything we had, but the truth is, we barely used most of what we owned. It was overcrowding our lives. When you live in a traditional home or apartment, you will usually have a few extra rooms to throw your junk in, and it's not going to affect your day-to-day routine, but when your house is only 400 square feet or less, that extra junk **WILL** affect your day-to-day routine. You will either need to find a clever storage solution or just get rid of it. Trust us when we say that you will get rid of most things eventually; if we did it all over again, we would have done it sooner rather than later. Once you finally pare down, you will only own things that are important and meaningful in your life. It is so much easier to remember where you left an item if you don't have so many to keep track of to begin with.

Time spent housekeeping will be drastically reduced. Oh what a shame, right? No one likes cleaning—well, some may, and there is nothing wrong with that. This was a major benefit of our tiny house. It may not take five minutes to clean like some people have claimed, but it sure takes a lot less than it did in our old, big house. Vacuuming and sweeping only take a few minutes, and the smaller footprint of the rest of the house makes deep cleaning so much easier.

It is easier to stay organized. With less stuff, each "thing" has its place, and therefore it is much easier to keep tidy. But your personality traits will play a big role in this; if you tend to be unorganized like we are it can be quite a learning curve to get organized, but the plus side is that you can adapt quicker when you have to.

Decorating Costs Much Less

Painting is one of the easiest ways to drastically change an interior or exterior look, and also one of the cheapest. With a tiny house, it is no longer daunting to change the paint colors in a "room" or the whole space. Before we moved out of our last rental, we needed to paint the house back to the boring drab colors it was before, and we can still remember that horrible week of never-ending painting—it felt like it went on forever! In our tiny house we have changed the paint colors a few times and added some accent walls. It took really two days tops. And most little projects like painting the bathroom or kitchen are a few hours at best. Plus, the cost: we used a lot less paint than we did with any other house because, well, the house is tiny! The same thing goes with decorating and furniture. Many people choose to build their own custom storage couches or built-in furniture to utilize space best, but we wanted real furniture, just smaller in size. Shopping for smaller pieces saves a lot of money, and since you interact with everything in your house so much more often, you may desire to switch things around regularly like we do. In the first few years living in our tiny house, we went through three couches alone. If something doesn't work or you get bored with it, you can get rid of it or sell it instead of just sticking it in another room. Our house is always evolving and changing, and that is one of our favorite parts of tiny living: we can actually afford to redecorate regularly!

A More Intimate And Cozy Home

Larger homes, such as the average size American house, have gigantic rooms; tiny houses have tiny rooms. There is no sense of intimacy and coziness in a room big enough to hold a football team. The smaller, or shall we say "fun-sized" rooms of a tiny house are cozy and more comfortable when designed right, and the small space gives a sense of intimacy that you can't easily replicate in a large home.

Tiny Houses Are Unique

Every tiny house is a reflection of the owner who built it or had it built. There are no cookie-cutter tiny houses, and that is just one of the many beautiful things about them; we are all unique, and our tiny houses should be a reflection of our needs, wants, and desires.

There are truly endless benefits to simplifying your life and downsizing to a tiny house, and as we are all individuals, we will all react to things differently. A benefit we have truly enjoyed is it gets you closer to the ones you love and share your little home with. You will work on your communication and become more in sync with each other. Starting with a healthy relationship is key as outlined in the previous chapter; building a good foundation for your relationship and honing those qualities in a small space with your spouse or family provides you benefits that money can never buy.

Rewards & Benefits of Downsizing

- Save lots of money!
- Create freedom
- Less stress worrying about paying high cost bills
- Ability to live mortgage-free!
- Less stuff to clean
- Less stuff to keep organized
- Freedom to travel
- You can take it traveling anywhere
- Cheaper to redecorate
- Build in an environmentally-friendly way
- Cost of building a tiny house is much less than a traditional house
- Use less energy and resources
- Live a decluttered life
- Intimate and cozy
- Unique living

Challenges

Limited Space For Things

A nice way to transition into the challenges of tiny house living is to mention something that is also one of its greatest benefits: when you live in a tiny house, you will constantly assess what you own and what you are bringing into the space. When you go out shopping and you see something you would just normally buy for your house, you really have to think about where you are going to put it. Even down to a pair of shoes or another shirt. Will it be replacing something? What will it replace? Space in a tiny house comes at a premium, but there are still opportunities to have all you need in a tiny house. Our home is 374 square feet, and we have most everything we needed and wanted in our old house. We have bigger than average tiny house closets, we have lots of shoes, lots of jackets, lots of dress clothes, and lots of other items, but even with ample storage in our home, we still have to seriously think about and consider what we buy and bring into the home. You just can't stick something in an extra room or closet and deal with it later. You pretty much have to deal with it right away (or you can keep it in your car for a little bit until you clear room). This may seem like a challenge and it certainly is, but it will really help you gain a perspective on the things you allow in your life and how they will impact you every day.

Limited Space For People
Living in a small space takes some adjustment when you are flying solo; add a couple of people into the mix and it will change the dynamic and all will need to learn the tiny house dance of interacting and getting around each other. It takes time, but you will soon learn to duck and weave with your partner in your day-to-day activities. When one of us is in the second loft getting dressed or putting away clothes, the other may be in and out of the bathroom which is under the loft. In our tiny house design, we utilized the sliding bathroom door with ladder rungs so it had access to the upper loft. If that door is open, the person upstairs can't get down. This is one of those things we have been conscious so we close the door so the other can get back down. It is all about teamwork when living with others in a small space, and as time goes on, you get better and better and you end up knowing the other's habits so well that this sloppy dance turns into a well-crafted ballet.

The Dog Days Of Summer
Depending on your climate and your personality, the different seasons of the year may bring additional challenges. In Northern California where we live, we have a pretty moderate climate, but in the summer months, we can easily get temperatures well above 100 degrees Fahrenheit. We always try to be conscious of our energy usage, but when it gets that hot, it's time to call up a friend who has a pool or close all the windows, draw

the blinds, and crank the A/C. When installing an A/C system in your tiny house, we highly recommend thinking about the location where you will install the inside head or unit. In our tiny house, we placed the inside unit right above the "living room," which is great when you are downstairs, but not so great when you are in bed at night and trying to sleep and it's still very hot. If we planned our A/C system all over again, we would have added a second interior unit or "head" to our mini split system for the sleeping loft. Since we can't really add that after the fact that easily, we purchased a small portable A/C unit we bring up in the loft in the summertime to keep us cool while we sleep, and then it goes into storage in the winter. Adding a skylight to your main loft that opens will also aid in keeping the upstairs cool and release some of that heat that will build up in the summer months. Cross-ventilation is also key no matter the square footage. In our 374-square foot space, we have eleven windows plus our 8-foot accordion window. We have opening windows on all four sides, which helps bring in fresh air no matter the season.

Cabin Fever: Winter Time

There is no set square footage required to develop cabin fever. You can get it in 200 square feet, you can get it in 2,000 square feet. We remember taking winter trips up to our friends' cabin in Lake Tahoe, snow falling by the inches. Although you have nowhere to go, you are content, enjoying the company with a fire blazing, playing games, and doing puzzles. After a few days go by, you really just want to get out and do something: sledding, grabbing some pizza, coffee, anything, anything at all. The feeling can get heightened in a very small space like a tiny house. Granted, everyone is different, but sometimes for us, the winter can be very challenging. When it is constantly raining and overcast, all you want to do is to be able to be outside, but you can't, it's not summer, it's not warm, it's cold, very cold. Add to the mix a couple of dogs with the frequent need to go outside, and it can get messy and disorganized quickly. We love the rain; we need it especially on the West Coast, but we still don't like being in it for too long. This is really the only time that a tiny house has felt very small, when a winter drags on way too long. Is this a deal breaker? Absolutely not; we just keep ourselves busier and get out of the house more.

Cabin Fever: Working From Home

This may not be a challenge at all for people who do not work at home, but we like to get out during the day and when the work day is over, we get to come home and start a fire in our tiny wood burning stove, make a cocktail, and cozy up on the couch. We think it is all a part of the learning process of living tiny. Some people may never get cabin fever; you may work all day and can't wait to get home, or you may work from home and by the time the work day is over, you just need to get out. We own our business and work from home (or anywhere with Internet). On days when we stay home all day and work, we definitely have some cabin fever creep in. It is also hard to stay focused on work when you are at home and chores or to-do lists creep up in the back of your mind. The best way we have felt to combat this feeling is to just get out. Go to a coffee shop or a park, get down to work, and when the day is over, we can't wait to get back to our little abode. Even on our "Tiny House" business trips after a few days, we can't wait to get back home to our tiny house. It is very much a part of us and we miss it.

Sickness In A Small Space

What if you get sick? Well, there is a good chance it's gonna happen. Whether you sleep in a loft or on the main floor, it's good to either have an alternative space to sleep in on the main floor to be close to the bathroom or bring a little trash bag up with you to the loft so you don't have to climb up and down stairs when you are feeling ill. The times we have been sick in our tiny house are no more frequent then in our previous big houses.

Comfortable Couch

We cannot stress this enough: get a comfortable couch. Yes, the custom built-in couches may look cool, but I have yet to see one or sit on one that was ACTUALLY comfortable. Storage is great, but you can't have storage EVERYWHERE. Plan your space for an actual couch, emphasis on comfort. It will get a lot of use, way more use than any couch in a previous house you lived in. Make sure it is comfy; otherwise, you will be shopping for another couch soon. We've done this song and dance several times and ended up spending more money than we ever thought we would on "testing" couches for six months or so at a time. Had we just saved our pennies and purchased the couch we knew we originally wanted and knew was comfortable, we could have saved ourselves the hassle and headache and money.

Trips To The Loo In The Middle Of The Night

Going to the bathroom in the middle of the night: nobody likes to do it, but it's not something you can usually prevent. In this case, we highly recommend building a staircase to go to the main loft or any loft that is used for sleeping. This makes the late night exits much easier to handle. Don't forget to have a proper handrail to guide you down in the dark!

Where To Park

Where do you park these so-called tiny homes? This may be one of the most common questions asked, and the options grow every week. Finding land to live on may take time and personal effort on the individual looking. It may involve ads on Craigslist, connecting with your neighbors, or even land hosting groups on Facebook. Many cities and counties all across the US are allowing tiny houses into their zoning, and some are even being known as tiny house-friendly cities. There are welcoming RV parks and tiny house communities popping up all over the country. The International Code Council even added in the international residential code for defining Tiny Houses, which provides a guide for local municipalities in allowing tiny houses in their local communities. No matter the challenges tiny houses used to face, there is no stopping this movement. The movement to simplify is something that resonates with countless people who are tired of pursuing that "American Dream" of bigger means better.

A Tiny House Still Needs Maintenance

Although small, a tiny house is still a house, and it will need repairs eventually just like a regular house. The only time you will never have to worry about doing repairs on your dwelling is when you're renting a home or an apartment, but we're trying to break free from all that, right? We want financial freedom! Maintenance is not a bad thing, it just comes with the territory. Whether it is a car, a relationship, or a house, it will need some TLC. We have done our fair share of maintenance on our home in the many years we have lived tiny. One of the bigger maintenance items we have undertaken to date was replacing the full exterior siding on our home. Several years after being built, our original wood T1-11 siding was developing rot on the backside of our house, so it all had to be removed. To ensure we would never have this problem again, we opted for an ultra-light aluminum siding called Knotwood to

fully clad our house. The beauty of this product is that they have over thirty different types of wood grains to choose from and limitless solid colors, so we chose Hickory wood grain and Deep Ocean matte. Now this was a much bigger than average project to undertake, but it needed to be done. While we could have just replaced it with the same original wood material, we decided to upgrade and learn from our mistakes and improve upon them. In addition to the new siding, we have done many other maintenance items around the house, including replacing fixtures, appliances, a water heater, and so on. It all just comes with the territory when you are a homeowner, a tiny home owner. On the plus side of this challenge, since your house is so small, the time invested in repairs, and most importantly the impact on the wallet, will only be a fraction of what it would be with an average-sized home.

The Top 10 Challenges of Downsizing:

- Limited space for your junk; we promise, it's a good thing
- Everyone needs their personal space, even in a tiny house
- Staying cool in summer with hot lofts
- Cabin fever during the cold winter days
- Working from home
- Dealing with sickness
- Comfortable furniture in a tiny house
- When nature calls
- Finding a spot to kick it
- A tiny house is still a house

CHAPTER 10

How Practical Is A Tiny House For The Long-Term?

TINY HOUSES HAVE BECOME A DREAM FOR MANY. Some are closer to living their tiny dream and some have it as a future plan. Regardless of when you plan on going tiny, at some point you'll likely wonder if they're really practical long-term or if you're being unreasonable to think you can live in such a small space for years to come and be content with it. Those thoughts rolled around in our head quite a bit before moving into our space. Since this was going to be a completely new experience for us and there weren't too many examples at the time of people who had lived in theirs for very long, we felt we were heading into unchartered waters and were taking a chance. Thankfully, many years have passed, and we can now speak from experience in hopes it'll be helpful to others.

So Is Living Tiny Really Practical Long-Term?

We would have to say with a strong conviction, YES! Many will have different reasons for going tiny. In our line of business, we talk to thousands of people from all walks of life with different dreams and goals for their tiny house. For some, it will be somewhat of a short-term goal,

maybe two to five years in order to pay off student loans or other debt to become debt-free (oh what an amazing feeling when you reach that goal). Some will want to have one for maybe five to ten years in order to cut living expenses so they can build or buy a larger house when they feel they've outgrown the tiny house. Some want to ultimately simplify and keep it small for years to come, to travel more and just keep a lower cost of living indefinitely. Some have even planned to only live tiny for a few years and have ended up surpassing that original goal with no intent of leaving the tiny life. Whatever your reasons or goal for going tiny, staying realistic with your expectations will not leave you disappointed. So what aspects exactly keep this dream a doable, long-term reality?

Aspects That Make Tiny Living Doable Long-Term

We've touched on these topics throughout the book, but we will restate these very important key points as they are the driving force to a successful transition. To make a tiny house practical long-term, it all depends on you and what you truly need.

1. Be (incredibly) realistic with your design:

It sounds simple enough, but really the designing phase can be a stressful time. With any move, home renovation, or structure, you will start to see dollar signs when figuring out everything you want and feel you need in your space. When we're looking at ways to be more efficient with the space in our home, we may start to cut out things or even the size of the space we ultimately want, and think we can manage with less. While we definitely believe in being reasonable—for instance, you may have to choose between having that awesome vintage cast iron claw foot tub and the load of tiles in both the kitchen and bathroom due to the weight of the materials, and it being built on a trailer (accounting for weight of materials is very important). But if you don't want to settle for a horse trough (which we love, by the way, but everyone's needs and styles are different) in place of a ceramic bathtub, then it would be wise to just save a bit longer and take that time in order to have what you feel you want or need.

Also be practical with the size you need, since this is an investment you don't want to treat lightly. Four to six feet smaller may sound great for your wallet, but don't settle if in the back of your mind you know that you really want and maybe even need a bit of a larger space. Four to six feet less may not sound like much in general housing, but in tiny houses, even 2 feet makes a HUGE difference. Once you build your tiny house on wheels, it will be nearly impossible to expand if you feel you need more space. The only other option at that point will be to build a separate tiny house as an addition. So if you're able to add to your budget in order to have the tiny house and size that you actually want, do it. Be patient, it will pay off in the long run.

2. Be (incredibly) realistic with yourself

You've likely seen a ton of tiny houses at this point, and they're usually staged and tidy in photos or videos. Yet, you're thinking and wondering how you're ever going to get to that point of minimalism or organization, and wondering if you can ever be one of those minimalists who can live in such a small space or if it's really for you. Don't worry, we were the same way and had those same feelings. And trust us, most (99 percent) who make this leap have these same fears. It's human, it's natural. But it's also important. As we've touched on earlier, we weren't sure if this lifestyle was going to be doable for us or not, long-term or at all. What we did know was that we were going to try to adapt tiny house living to our needs. We knew being minimalist wasn't our goal since it just wasn't in our nature. However, we had a strong desire for this lifestyle and knew no matter what we would adapt it to our needs. This is where being realistic with yourself is very important. Realizing what you actually need in order to make it work—whether that idea fits into others' opinions or not—you need to incorporate what works for you. Recognize your daily needs. Pay attention to the items that you use on a regular basis and what items make your life feel easier and comfortable. For instance, if you currently enjoy some solid TV/movie time and enjoy a comfy couch now and that's important to you, recognize that when downsizing, a built-in couch with thinner cushions may not cut it for you. Even if it does allow some storage, some things aren't worth sacrificing for your comfort. The list of variables

can go on and on; ultimately keep in mind that you need to be realistic with what you use on a daily or weekly basis, and working those items into your design will make for a comfortable transition.

3. Be (incredibly) realistic with your budget

When shopping for a car, the most important factor you will usually take into account is your budget. You will try to get all the features you need and want to work with the money you have in your pocket. Even if you plan to finance, you will still need to work with a realistic budget that will work for the length of the loan. When choosing a car, some people may be completely content with an air conditioner and heated seats. Those may satisfy all their needs; after all, a car may just be a means of transportation, the same with a tiny house. Some people may look at it with the mindset of just needing shelter and nothing else. Again with a car, air conditioning may be a feature that is expected but not enough to fulfill their needs; some people may want the car to go ahead and park itself so you don't even have to deal with the pain of parallel parking. There is no right or wrong way. It really comes down to preference and needs. Tiny houses are the same way. A simple shelter with limited plumbing and solar power may be perfect for many and roughing it for others. This very important factor is why there can be a wide price range for tiny houses. We have seen some as cheap as $15,000 for a small, basic tiny house on a 14-foot trailer, all the way well past $100,000 for a more luxurious tiny house with all the amenities. Just browse Tiny House Listings and you can see how much they vary. When calculating your budget, you will need to decide if you will be building it yourself or hiring a builder to construct it for you. You will be able to stretch your budget much farther if you are building it yourself versus hiring a contractor and paying him to build it for you. As most people know, it is quite expensive to hire a skilled builder, but it may work out much better for your situation if you already have a busy schedule with work. The majority of people choose to build their tiny houses themselves in an effort to learn and have the satisfaction of building their own home and, most importantly, to stretch their budget as much as possible. Once you figure out the ideal budget for you home, it is best to do a lot of research. Research what it costs to build a home similar to what you have in mind for your dream tiny

home. Browse the tiny house classified site we mentioned earlier to get a sense of what the market is for tiny homes. Ask other tiny home dwellers what would be a realistic price range for a home like theirs. The only place I would recommend not to include in any research is any tiny house TV show. These TV shows show unreal expectations for the true cost of tiny houses. The main objective for these tiny house TV shows is really to get viewers, which in turn creates ad revenue. These shows are great for entertainment and design ideas, but not for true actual cost. Take it from us, we were on one of these TV shows and they stated the full cost of our house was in reality just half of what the materials alone cost. For many people who have been a part of these TV shows, they have later had to sell their tiny dream home due to difficult circumstances and faced a backlash from people who claimed they watched the house get built on TV for much cheaper than the asking price. This effect has really skewed the idea of the true cost of what tiny homes cost, and therefore you may get quite a shock when you are expecting your budget to stretch much farther than it really can. Anything custom can be expensive, whether it is a tiny home or a one-of-a-kind piece of art; pricing can vary. When building your budget for you tiny home, really think long and hard about what is most important to you and what you can live without realistically.

Many things can always be added later if your budget is tight. Think about the bones of your build and what would be the best to have done right away. Windows, doors, and lofts are always good to have done right during the construction and can be very difficult and costly to add later. Items like built-in couches, higher end appliances, decks, and interior finishes can always be added later if they don't fit in your budget. A good rule of thumb is anything that is inside the walls or a part of the walls should be a priority, and all other things can be modified much easier later.

4. Be (incredibly) realistic with your needs

Being realistic with what you need can be a double-edged sword at times. Since we are all different and have different wants and routines, we are all going to need some different aspects in our tiny house. However, when it comes to going tiny, there is a limiting factor of what wants can be fulfilled due to the weight limitations of tiny houses on wheels. If you're building on a foundation, then this wouldn't apply, but for the most of us doing tiny houses on wheels, we will need to keep weight of items in mind. Since we do work with clients regularly in building their dream tiny house, we hear many different ideas of wants and desires. For example, some may want a large glass garage style window/door. While these are super cool looking and really add a unique look to a tiny house and also really open it up, they are very expensive, heavy, and not ideal for locations with fluctuating weather and temperatures, as there is no insulation on the large area that they take up. There are pros and cons to many things when going tiny. Making a list of wants initially, then looking at it and actually calculating the cost and the weight can help you better reach the decision as to what you really need and can afford. On the other hand, trying to go too extreme and thinking you can do with the bare minimum and feeling as though you will just adapt can be dangerous. Transitioning into a tiny house is a new experience and many of us aren't used to that size of a space. Being realistic with what you really do need and use daily will be extremely helpful in making the transition more flawless. One of the things we knew we needed was clothes storage. We had seen so many who had gotten their closets down to just a few items. While this seemed like a great goal for us, it wasn't realistic for us right

away, since we did need both regular and dress clothes. So, we worked to have our closet in the second loft. This space still provided plenty of storage for clothes and shoes and accessories. The trade-off is that we do have to climb a small ladder to get to them, and generally pick out our clothes and change down below. We have gotten used to it and it is second nature now, but it did take some adapting in the beginning. Many have asked us why we didn't just put the closet down on the bottom level and maybe have a smaller kitchen in order to have that space. For us, that wasn't a compromise we were willing to make; having a good-sized kitchen was important to us because we do entertain and needed lots of prepping space. So, having the closet in the second loft was a good compromise for us. There's always a little give and take when downsizing. By being realistic in what you need without feeling like you're sacrificing and giving up too much will help you get to a happy medium and ultimately a comfortable living situation in your tiny house.

Conclusion

If going tiny has been a dream of yours at any point in life, but you have some hesitations, take comfort in knowing that you're not alone and having hesitations is normal for any new situation. We felt those same thoughts of hesitation and doubt; it felt like something that would be a distant dream but not attainable anytime soon. One day we would live a more simplified life and would get to spend more time on the things we loved with the people we loved. What we didn't realize was how quickly it would all fall into place. Carefully considering your game plan and sharing your thoughts and dreams with a trusted confidant or close friend can help aid you in reaching your goal faster than you would have thought possible.

Talking things out with those you trust is always helpful, friends and family can provide a point of view that we may not have thought of and that can better prepare us to face any challenges that might come up, "Plans fail when there is no consultation, but there is accomplishment through many advisers." –Proverbs 15:22. We couldn't have done this journey alone. We relied on the support and input of many in our family and friends, even when they may not have been able to do it themselves, but they saw how much this meant to us. Add hard work and careful planning, along with selling off unused or unnecessary items that didn't contribute to our life and goals in any way, and we found ourselves living a life that we could have never imagined. Oftentimes we look around and say, "I can't believe we did it!" Who knew we would ever be in this type of situation and loving it. More importantly, who knew that we could be SO much more satisfied and happy with much less.

The savings in money, and more importantly in our time and sanity, has made this adventure worth every stressful moment in the beginning. It's made those doubtful questions of whether we can do this or not worth it. It's made every little unexpected adjustment and every nerve-racking moment worth it all. We still can't believe that we have the privilege of living this simplified lifestyle and can't believe what peace of mind it has brought us. We can't encourage enough going tiny and simplifying if this is something that you have personally been contemplating.

The risk and the fear are all worth the end result if you take the time to carefully plan as much as you can. It will be an adjustment; it won't always be smooth and easy throughout the whole process, but generally speaking, nothing worth having is. Take the step and enjoy the benefits of a more simplified lifestyle. It is not just about the tiny house; the tiny house is just one of the great tools in the process of simplifying, a tool to craft a more meaningful life. We are all individuals and we all have different needs, and a tiny house to us is not one set of strict guidelines. It can be anything you need it to be. How much you downsize is up to you. The goal of this book is to help guide you to a way that can free up some time so you can focus your life on what is most important to you.

AFTERWORD

Our Tiny House Trailers and Tiny House Shells

WE MANUFACTURE our industry-leading tiny house trailers in four locations across the United States; we also ship to all fifty states and Canada. We also build our custom tiny house shells in several locations across the country. Our tiny house trailers are truly custom and available from 10 to 50 feet in standard decks, drop axles, and deck overs, bumper pull, goosenecks, and fifth wheel hitches. We will offer you insight and knowledge on what is most important in your tiny house trailer foundation, and show you the practical options you may need to make your build successful. We have an extensive background in tiny house trailers, tiny houses, metal fabrication, and interior design. We design and sell the "#1 Tiny House Trailers Available from Manufacturers that Have Been Building High Quality Trailers for over 30 Years." As tiny house people ourselves, our number one goal is to help others going tiny and to simplify that process and save you money right off the bat. Every trailer is custom built for you just the way you want it; we will never try to sell you what's "in stock." Each trailer is built just for you. We will guide you throughout the whole process to design the best tiny house trailer to fit your needs. Even after the trailer is picked up and the building

begins, we are always available as a resource for our customers, and we have a very easily accessible social media presence. You can start your tiny house journey by requesting a free quote on our website at www.TinyHouseBasics.com.

Why We Remodeled The Exterior Of Our Tiny House

When we built our tiny house in late 2014, we used a popular and affordable exterior siding called T1-11. This is a plywood siding that comes in 10-foot lengths and allowed us to use full length sheets between the upper and lower 2x12 lumber we used as a base trim on our tiny house. T1-11 requires a good amount of maintenance and sealing from the elements at least every two years, but that was not soon enough for us on our tiny house. In less than two years, we were already developing rot on our T1-11 on the backside of our house, and this is even in the moderate climate of the San Francisco Bay Area. We could not have imagined what it would be like in a wetter climate!

Now what? Well, we knew it needed to be replaced sooner rather than later, and since our tiny house is built on a trailer, it needed to be lightweight. Now, T1-11 is not a really lightweight material, but if we did change it out, we knew we needed to try and cut down on any weight if possible, and we also needed a material that would last much longer than two years. Our search started with the basic parameters of lightweight and a long life. Shortly after our search started, we stumbled upon Knotwood Aluminum products. Immediately these products stood out to us because of their wood-like appearance, yet it was actually aluminum. Knotwood aluminum finishing gives you the beauty and warmth of wood without the time-consuming maintenance. They use a process called sublimation that has been tested all over the world for durability. This is a completely modular system that uses hidden fastening systems to give you a beautiful and seamless look when the installation is done. Most importantly to us, it is lightweight, low maintenance, and has the high durability qualities of aluminum while maintaining the natural beauty and warm-textured feel of timber.

In addition to these features, it is also green-certified and non-combustible, which is ideal for any home, especially a tiny home into which we poured our blood, sweat, and tears. For our new exterior design, we decided to go with two tones of Knotwood. We chose the solid color Blue Ocean Matte for the majority of the tiny house and chose the wood grain Hickory for an accent wall above and below the accordion window and also underneath the soffits on both ends. After we removed all the old exterior siding and patched up the nail holes in our vapor wrap, we were ready for the installation of our new Knotwood siding. There was a little bit of a learning curve working with the aluminum pieces, but we quickly got the hang of it and actually preferred working with Knotwood over wood products for siding. The hidden fastening systems made the finished product look perfect, and we are in no way professionals when it comes to siding! We also saved an estimated 900 pounds in weight over our old heavy T1-11 exterior siding. The beautiful finished look of Knotwood cannot be compared to any other building material we have seen before, and will ensure our tiny house looks great for years to come with very little maintenance. It's really hard to believe when you see it

in person that it is not wood, it is aluminum! For more information on Knotwood siding and decking, please check out www.Knotwood.com.

On-Grid vs. Off-Grid Power

How do you choose whether you want to power your tiny house with grid power or solar power? Sometimes you may not have a choice. First off, it is good to take in account where your tiny house will be parked. If you plan to travel and stay at RV parks, you will most likely have access to on-grid power; you may even have grid power already on the land where you plan to live, like we did. If you plan to park your tiny house in a more remote area, you will likely need to have some alternate power source, like a generator or solar power, and then the choice gets much easier. When we built our tiny house in 2014, we were on unimproved land in a small city in the San Francisco Bay Area. We didn't have much sunlight exposure and no grid power to use, so we were forced to use generators to power our tiny house. Even with a small energy-efficient Honda generator it got old quick; your ears would get fatigued from hearing the constant whirring of a generator. After a short period of a few weeks, we knew we needed to find a new home with some sun exposure for our own sanity. We knew we just needed sunlight, whether it was on-grid or off-grid. It didn't matter at that point. When we moved our tiny house to our new home, we were fortunate to have grid power already there and ready to hook up to our house. This made it much easier to transition to life in a tiny house. Now, of course our energy usage was much less by default because our house was so small. As the years passed, the desire to be fully off-grid started growing. We have great sun exposure, high-efficiency appliances, and we use all LED bulbs inside our tiny house, so we're pretty much ready for solar, right? Well, not exactly; it's a bit more than just switching out light bulbs and appliances. Over the past year, we have been slowly preparing ourselves for the move to be more energy-efficient. Here are a few things we recommend doing when you are considering switching over to solar power:

- Educate yourself. This is the most important step and should always be the first. Take your time and learn the facts about the true cost and impact of switching to solar power. One of our favorite resources and suppliers is www.Altestore.com. They have many valuable resources, videos, and articles to help prepare you for switching over to solar power.
- Start conserving energy now! It will take time to truly know how you use power and what your consumption and habits may be as the seasons change. Start by switching out your lightbulbs to LED bulbs and think about what type of appliances you plan to use in your tiny house and what their efficiency is like. You may score a great deal on some used appliances, but if they are older and less energy-efficient, it can cost you more in the long run. Think about the insulation you plan to use in your tiny house; the energy-efficiency will greatly impact how much energy you use to heat and cool your home. It may be more expensive in the beginning, but a well-sealed tiny house will save you a lot on heating and cooling.
- Calculate your average energy usage with a solar calculator. A solar calculator helps you size the battery bank, watts of solar panels, and

the solar charge controller you need for your off-grid system. You can find one on the website we mentioned above. This method will help you build a system that gets you through the average amount of sunlight in the least sunny month of the year for your geographical location.

Off-Grid Pros

- Low monthly cost to operate after initial investment
- You can truly live anywhere you please; location is not dependent on how close to a grid connection you are
- Switching to renewable energy can lessen global emissions
- Power wherever you go, especially if you plan to travel with your tiny house
- Power outages won't affect you
- Off-grid land prices are cheaper than those with grid power
- Using only the energy you generate forces you to be energy-efficient
- Independence: you will never be subjected to rate hikes from grid power systems

Off-Grid Cons

- Initial cost for equipment and installation
- Solar energy generation slows drastically in cloudier places
- You may exceed the amount of power the renewable energy system provides
- Living off-grid requires a lifestyle change
- You are your own utility company; you will need to monitor your usage, always
- If the panels are built on the roof of your tiny house, you may have to reposition your house with the change of seasons

Products We Love For Our Tiny House:

- **Knotwood -** Our beautiful new aluminum siding that is lightweight, non-combustible, no rot worries, eco-friendly, green-certified, and will look brand-new for many, many years to come.

- **Rooftop tent by Freespirit Recreation -** These high-quality roof top tents are a must for any camper and off-roader. They're easy and quick to set up and can withstand extreme weather. Our lives when out in the middle of nowhere wouldn't be the same without them.

- **goTenna -** These off-grid communication devices help us stay in contact with each other when hiking or camping. It's an off-grid communication tool to keep in touch with others when you don't have service. We love to be off-grid, but we also like to be safe and in touch with others for any possible emergencies. Having that ability to keep in touch with your group for safety brings peace of mind.

- **Trailer valet -** This tool has been one of our most used; we use it to move tiny house trailers and tiny house shells in and out of our shop and maneuver them around in tight spaces.

- **EcoloBlue -** They supply atmospheric water generators. We have the maximum-efficiency alkaline model in our storage closet; it removes the humidity in the air and filters it through a five stage filtration process and produces up to eight gallons of clean drinking water a day, perfect for off-grid living.

- **On the go portable water softener -** Having soft water is important and gentle on our skin and hair, but more importantly for a tiny house, it's gentle on the plumbing and fixtures. This little gem has saved much wear and tear on both our plumbing and appliances, as well as our hair and skin. These portable water softeners are designed for RVs, tiny homes, and boats, and are easy to pack up and travel with.

- **eTrailer -** This has been our go-to source for towing, trailer parts, and accessories for over ten years. They have a wealth of informational articles for all things related to trailers, towing, and vehicle needs. By far the best customer service around, they have been a valuable resource for us and our tiny house trailer customers.

- **Eheat, our small heating panel behind our couch -** This very slim heating panel has been an awesome heater to offset the high energy usage of our mini split heat pump. At a low usage of only 400 watts, this little heater is perfect for small spaces and individual rooms in a regular-sized house. The low energy usage allows you to leave the unit on all the time to keep any room a comfortable temperature

- **Finex cast iron pans -** The best cast iron pans you'll ever own! We love these cooking tools more than someone should love cast iron. They're of the highest quality and made in Portland, Oregon. These are our main pans that we cook daily with. Plus, they look cool with their unique design.

- **Flor carpet tiles -** We love that these carpet tiles come in 12- to-16- inch squares, making it easy to create your own design and have the size you need vs. a rug that's too large or too small. You can cut them to any size and shape and they're extremely durable. We've used these throughout our tiny house in the main living area, as well as our master loft and second loft.

- **Retract-A-Gate pet gate -** This is another thing we use every day and has made our life much easier. This low profile rolled up pet gate is a must for anyone with pets or babies to keep them contained in an area.

- **Happy Habitat throws -** These throws are the best! They're soft and made from recycled cotton. (The owner explains what that is on her website.) On top of being solid-made throws with some nice weight to them, her designs are excellent. These throws are statement pieces on top of being comfortable to snuggle up in.

- **Original Nomad Portable Hot Tubs -** Who doesn't like hot tubs? We know we are all about them, but most are big and bulky and cost a lot of money to operate. These portable hot tubs can be set up in minutes and brought anywhere you go, especially camping or to a family cabin like we did. You can heat up the water with propane in the specially designed coil system, or even start a wood burning fire if you don't have access to propane. These have taken camping to a new level for us!

- **Black's Farmwood –** After much searching, we found incredible one-hundred-year-old tobacco barn oak reclaimed floors that we will be replacing our not-so-great laminate floor with. In a small space, having eco-friendly materials is important to the air quality in tighter quarters. Black's Farmwood specializes in reclaimed and sustainable wood. With lots of non-reputable companies out there taking advantage of the reclaimed trend, these guys are legit and have an amazing showroom with large samples on the floor so you can actually visualize what your space will look like.

- **Microfridge Combo Microwaves and Refrigerators -** These small combo units are great for small spaces, utilizing only one plug. The refrigerator plugs into the back of the microwave and the microwave then plugs into the wall. The microwave also has a built-in smoke alarm and two 120v outlets on the front to charge your gadgets.

Tiny House Websites We Love:

- **www.TinyHouseBasics.com:** This is our site, so of course it's our favorite. You can request a free tiny house trailer or shell quote right on our website and learn even more about tiny house living.

- **www.TinyHouseBlog.com:** The ultimate blog for tiny houses.

- **www.TinyHouseListings.com:** The global marketplace for tiny houses.

- **www.tinyrevolution.us:** Tiny r(E)volution is a media-mentary on their goal to downsize, minimize, prioritize, and proselytize the plight of the Tiny House in a sustainable world. Along the way they share their personal stories, tales of discovery, and a lot more information.

- **www.youtube.com/user/relaxshacksDOTcom:** "RelaxshacksDOTcom" is hosted by Derek "Deek" Diedricksen, former host of HGTV's "Tiny House Builders" and "Extreme Small Spaces", and author of "Humble Homes, Simple Shacks", and "Microshelters". Deek and his brother Dustin travel the US touring and filming tiny houses, and more, as they build and design their own works (often featured) at the same time.

For permission requests, please contact the publisher at:
Mango Publishing Group
2850 Douglas Road, 3rd Floor
Coral Gables, FL 33134 USA
info@mango.bz

For special orders, quantity sales, course adoptions and corporate sales, please email the publisher at sales@mango.bz. For trade and wholesale sales, please contact Ingram Publisher Services at customer.service@ ingramcontent.com or +1.800.509.4887.

Tiny House Basics: Living the Good Life in Small Spaces

Library of Congress Cataloging Number: 2017937999
ISBN: (paperback) 978-1-63353-571-8, (ebook) 978-1-63353-572-5
BISAC category code HOM023000 HOUSE & HOME / Small Spaces.

Printed in the United States of America